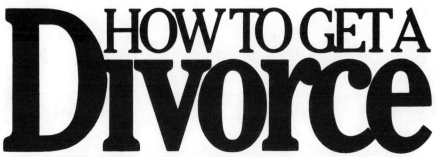

HOW TO GET A
Divorce

A practical handbook for residents of the District of Columbia, Maryland, and Virginia who are contemplating separation and divorce.

By Sandra Kalenik

Second Edition
Published by
The Washington Book Trading Company

The Author   *Sandra Kalenik* is a writer with offices in Washington, D.C. She has written on various aspects of the law for a variety of publications, and on divorce for the *The Washington Post* and *The Washingtonian.* She resides in Luray, Virginia.

Published by The Washington Book Trading Company
PO Box 1676
Arlington Va. 22210
Nancy Carter Modrak, Books Editor

For you, the reader.

Acknowledgements
I wish to thank Jay S. Bernstein, J.D., who practices law in the District of Columbia and Maryland, and who was the coauthor of the first edition of this book. His continued support and knowledge have been invaluable.

Also, Valerie Szabo, J.D., who practices family law in Alexandria, Virginia, whose efforts and knowledge on the Virginia section of the book have not gone unnoticed.

Contents

Preface

Since this book was first published in 1976, there have been several changes in the divorce laws of the District of Columbia, Maryland, and Virginia. Most notably, the District of Columbia has abolished all of its "fault" grounds for divorce, which included adultery and desertion. The grounds now are separation without cohabitation (voluntary or nonvoluntary).

The legislators in Maryland removed impotency as a ground, and lowered the waiting period for involuntary separation without cohabitation from three years to two. The State also adopted the "Family Use Personal Property Act," which can have far-reaching repercussions regarding property settlements. This Act is covered in the chapter on Property.

In Virginia, six months of voluntary separation without cohabitation was added as a ground, provided that there are no minor children and there is a valid separation agreement between the parties.

Residency requirements also have changed some. In the District of Columbia, it's now six months and it's also six months in Virginia for the aforementioned ground.

That's a brief note on the legal side of divorce law changes. The book contains many more. Other changes also have occured which are not as definitive perhaps as the changing of grounds. Many of these changes have occurred as a result of the Equal Rights Amendment, a form of which was adopted by all three jurisdictions. The most common theme that has resulted from state-passed Equal Rights Acts is that the husband and wife are equal partners in a marriage and, as such, they have equal rights and responsibilities. The most notable example of this is the switch from using the terms "husband" and "wife" to the nongender "spouse." Two notable side effects of this are that the "spouse" is responsible for assisting the dependent spouse with support payments, regardless of gender; and both spouses are responsible for the financial support of the children. Consequently, the role of women in divorce has more active consequences.

Also as a result of ERA, the legislators have given women more equal legal status by recognizing the value of their homemaking services as much as their wage-earning spouses. Homemaking services are now taken into consideration by the court in determining support payments as well as marital property settlements. The wife's nonmonetary role has a major, recognized value.

Another result is that where once judges abided by what was called "the tender years," doctrine which meant that the mother was considered to be the natural custodian of the young children, this is not necessarily the case now. As a Maryland statute says, "In any custody proceeding, neither parent shall be given preference solely because of his or her sex."

One very good change that seems to have taken place, is that court clerks seem to be more helpful now in assisting do-it-yourselfers with their divorce cases.

A word about case law. There are specific statutes which govern divorce laws, but how they are applied may be another story. A judge may take into account mitigating or special circumstances and rule on those circumstances. This becomes case law. Case law, for example, can be a ruling in the wife's favor that the husband's child support payments made directly to the children and not to her as the court ordered, did not comply with his obligation.

Case law is important for two reasons. One, it is just as binding as the statutes. And two, it shows that no statute or law is so absolute, that particular circumstances cannot be taken into account.

Finally, this book is intended to be useful and practical; to assist you through the legal entanglements of divorce; and to help ease a painful period of life. We hope it serves you well—and your comments and suggestions for future editions will be appreciated.

Sandra Kalenik

Part 1: Do You Need A Lawyer?

For the majority of people, divorce is a traumatic experience. Not only are there feelings of pain, recrimination, guilt, and uncertainty, there also are all the problems that can go with a new life-style. You have to learn to live alone again, to adjust to a change of finances, to be a single parent responsible for decisions once made jointly, or to see your children only on visitation days. There is the added strain of dividing your accumulated possessions. Along with it all comes the legal problems of the divorce itself.

Divorce is first and foremost a lawsuit. One spouse has to charge the other spouse in an adversary proceeding authorized by a court of law. Regardless of how private you are or would like to be about your personal problems, you must spell out the facts to a judge or a judicial intermediary in order to obtain a divorce. The most common course is to hire a lawyer, tell him or her the facts, and hope for the best.

1

When a Lawyer Is Absolutely Necessary

If you have a lot of personal property, children, a home, if you are a woman and have not been working, or if you and your spouse are having difficulty deciding who gets what and how much money should be given for child support and alimony, then your best recourse is to see an attorney. An attorney is familiar with the laws of domestic relations, under which divorces fall. But more than that, an attorney can offer you the objective treatment your case might need, particularly if you and your spouse are arguing over everything from cars to toothpicks. A lawyer can advise you of things that you not only do not think about, but that you probably do not even know about.

Choosing a Lawyer

Most people don't think about lawyers until they are in trouble and need one. Then there is often a panic stage—what do I do, where do I go, where can I find one, whom should I get—accompanied by a lot of phone calls to friends and to family, or even by a quick run-down in the yellow pages.

It is extremely important that you choose a competent, interested attorney: one with whom you feel comfortable and who returns your phone calls, answers your questions directly, and is not always "too busy."

In choosing a lawyer, your best bet is to ask divorced friends whom they recommend and why. Ask them about what kind of work their lawyer has done for them, how much time the lawyer invested in the case, the outcome, and how much they were charged. Or ask an attorney to recommend someone if he or she does not do divorce work.

You can also go to a library and get a copy of Martindale-Hubbell's *Law Directory*. This book provides information on the lawyer's education, specialty, experience, and assets, and even provides a rating on competence. It's a good way to check the names of attorneys you get either from friends or referral services, although not all lawyers are listed.

You might consider going to the following places to find an attorney to help with your divorce. Check your local directory or information to find the phone numbers.

District of Columbia
> Lawyer Referral Service—Bar Association of the District of Columbia
> Neighborhood Legal Service Program, Family Law Section (Note: Accepts people only with net in-

come of $72 per week plus an allowance of $20 for each dependent.)

Maryland
    Lawyer Referral Service of the Montgomery County Bar Association
    Lawyer Referral Service of the Prince George's County Bar Association
    Legal Aid Bureau of Bowie
    Legal Aid Bureau of Prince George's County
    Legal Aid Bureau of Montgomery County
    Legal Assistance of Prince George's County
    Lawyer Referral Service, Bar Association of Baltimore City
    Legal Aid Bureau of Baltimore

Virginia
    Legal Aid Society of Arlington County
    Arlington Bar Association
    Alexandria Legal Aid
    Fairfax Lawyer Referral
    Lawyer Referral Service, Norfolk and Portsmouth Bar Association
    Lawyer Referral Service of Richmond
    Legal Aid Bureau of Richmond
    Lawyer Referral Service of Roanoke
    Legal Aid Society of Roanoke

Referral Services

Most referral services will charge you an initial fee of approximately $25 to $35 for a half-hour consultation with an attorney. After that, the fee is between you and the attorney. The attorney may charge you a flat rate, or by the hour. In either case, plan on spending $800 and up—more if there is property to be settled and there are children.

Legal Aid Societies

Legal aid societies may handle divorce cases, but only for the poor. Their requirements vary by counties and offices. But as a whole, they do not like to take divorce cases and often will not do them.

Who Pays Lawyer Fees

Attorney's fees can be expensive, especially if your divorce is contested. An attorney has only two products for sale: time and experience. Usually, your lawyer will require a retainer fee, ranging from a low of $500 to a high of $3,500. The retainer is based on whether the case is contested or

3

uncontested, the amount of property involved, how much time will be involved, what issues are in dispute, whether there is a custody battle or a fight over the amount of child support payments or alimony. In a hotly contested divorce case, fees could run as high as $10,000 to $25,000.

Deciding who pays those legal fees could be a battle in itself—and often is. Each person could pay for his or her own attorney, the husband could be required to pay all fees, or the party at fault in a contested case could be ordered to pay. Basically, it's another item that should be negotiated by your attorney.

Taxes and Lawyers Fees

There is some small relief when it comes to your legal fees. All of the time spent conversing with your lawyer that relates directly to taxes is deductible from your income taxes. If your lawyer charges $75 an hour and you spend three hours talking about your taxes and future tax status, you can deduct $225.

Being Your Own Lawyer

This book is not intended to recommend that you do your own divorce. However, in today's increasingly do-it-yourself world, more and more people are beginning to handle their own divorce proceedings, which is known as *pro se*. But be careful. It is not advisable for anyone with a lot of property and children to proceed without counsel. You are likely to end up with more regrets than you might now feel about your marriage. Also, judicial intermediaries who hear uncontested divorce cases and court clerks who may have to help you along the way are not always pleased and helpful with people doing their own divorce. But if you and your spouse have not been married very long, are amiable about the divorce, do not have much property, feel that you could divide your possessions yourself, do not have children, then you might find it to your advantage to be your own lawyer. It can save you money, although it may take you longer. It also can test the limits of your patience.

Is It Legal to Be Your Own Lawyer?

The Supreme Court has ruled that everyone has a right to the very best legal defense possible. People have the right to represent themselves in any type of case, unless a judge rules otherwise. Judges can order you to do just about everything from taking your hat off in court to hiring an attorney. And their orders are inviolable. If you disagree or if you don't follow a judge's order, you could be held for contempt of court. But the answer is, "Yes, it is legal to be your own lawyer."

The Trouble With Being Your Own Lawyer

There are problems with trying to be your own divorce lawyer, as there are in all legal cases. There are certain court procedures that must be followed in a divorce case, one of which, for example, is known as service. Service has to be administered in the correct legal manner; if it is not, a divorce can be rescinded, or you might have to go back and file a new action. Also, you have to be certain that everything that is necessary for your divorce case is in its file. Then there are important considerations, such as whether or not you will have a separation agreement and whether it is to be incorporated into your divorce action, which can make a big difference later on; whether alimony rights are to be waived; whether you are in the proper jurisdiction; and whether you fulfill all the legal requirements for getting a divorce. Even if you are firm about doing your own divorce, it would be best to check with a lawyer to make sure that you have everything in order. Also, a lawyer could give you advice suited to your particular circumstances.

Finally, laws do change, and you need to be certain that you have current and accurate information.

Mediation: the Legal Alternative

What Mediation Is

Until the last five years or so, just about the only alternative for divorcing couples was to hire a lawyer to do battle for them. Often the spouses would not even speak with each other, "communicating" only through their attorneys. And attorneys proliferated. There is now one lawyer for every 400 Americans. The addition of "no fault" to divorce laws has given rise to an emerging alternative for divorcing couples: mediation. Mediation is the process in which the divorcing couple work out their problems, disagreements, and marital issues with a trained, impartial third party—the mediator. The mediator assists the couple in resolving their differences in a constructive way to reach a "win-win" decision rather than the adversative "win-lose" situation.

The Mediators

Mediators may be social workers, psychologists, or lawyers trained in family and divorce mediation. At present, mediation is still so new that it is open turf for one of the above three professions to claim. At any rate, the mediator should receive formal training from a recognized program or institute. They are versed in family budgeting, the law, tax consequences of divorce, and a variety of options and alternatives crucial to contemplating divorce.

How Mediators Can Help

The major differences between mediators and lawyers are that mediators assist the couple in working out their disagreements between themselves; emphasize the restructuring of the family from a practical point of view, in addition to the legal side; pay more attention to the divorcing couple's emotional needs; and, they are impartial, representing neither the husband nor the wife, but both. Unlike the legal adversary system, mediation is sensitive to the integrity of the marriage and the future of the lives of the divorcing couples. It tries to build on the strengths of the relationship, avoiding the "we'll get him/her" so common with the adversary position.

How Mediation Works

As one mediator describes the process, "Mediation is neither therapy, nor the law—it's an educational process." The couple attends an orientation session in which the mediator thoroughly explains the rules of mediation such as what the couple should focus on, how they should speak to each other (keep raised voices down), and so on. The session usually lasts for two hours.

After the initial session, the couple attend five to eight two-hour sessions in which the mediator will guide them to make their own decisions on how they wish to end their marriage. They analyze their budgets and needs, divide marital property, review their children's needs, and reorganize their family and lifestyle to fit its new structure.

Mediators place special emphasis on providing an acceptable form of continuity where children are concerned, and may even include children in the sessions if warranted.

The process allows the parties to analyze their situations and to understand each other's needs as well as those of the children. It may alleviate the anger and bitterness that the couples initially may feel towards each other. It also makes the couple realize that although they may not be husband and wife, they are still parents. It encourages cooperation with each other in determining their relationship with their children.

Once the couple decides on what it is that they wish to do, the mediator draws up a statement that specifies what issues have been resolved. This statement is then given to the couple's respective attorneys who will draw up a formal separation agreement based on the statement.

The Cost of
Mediation

The cost of mediation varies, generally between $40 to $80 a session. It usually is requested that both parties contribute to the costs, eliminating any possible feelings that the one who pays may be getting preferred treatment. Sessions also may be held with co-mediators, a lawyer and a social worker, for example. These sessions can cost up to $120.

Does
Mediation
Work?

Statistics show that court-ordered child support and alimony payments tend to lag after two years, and tend to be ignored entirely after five years. Experience so far has shown that people tend to abide by agreements reached through mediation.

Where to
Get
Mediation
Assistance

The following is a partial list of places to turn to in locating mediators. You also should check with your local state bar associations which may have special mediation programs set up, such as Montgomery County Bar Association's "Voluntary Arbitration" program.

American Arbitration Association
1730 Rhode Island Avenue, N.W.
Washington, D.C.

Family and Child Associates
414 Hungerford Drive.
Rockville, Md.

Family Mediation Association
804 D Street, N.E.
Washington, D.C.

Family Mediation of Greater Washington
1515 N. Court Street
Arlington, Va.

Family Mediation Service
6817 Market Square Drive
McLean, Va.
         and
918 16th Street, N.W.
Washington, D.C.

Federal Mediation & Conciliation Service
2100 K Street, N.W.
Washington, D.C.

National Institute for Dispute Resolution
1901 L Street, N.W.
Washington, D.C.

National Legal Resource Center for Child Advocacy and
   Protection
c/o American Bar Association
1800 M Street, N.W.
Washington, D.C.

Grounds for Divorce And Annulment

The same trio involved in your marriage play a role in your divorce: you, your spouse, and the state. You can't simply break up, saddle your charger, and ride off into halcyon horizons. You have to give the state an acceptable reason why you should be allowed to break up. The reason is known as the ground for your divorce, and over the years each state has enacted legislation that governs acceptable grounds. If you don't meet the grounds, then—like it or not—you stay married. But don't despair. No legal definition or law is absolute. The application of law can vary, waiver, change, and can be molded to fit your particular case. In the District of Columbia you can obtain a "no fault" divorce on the grounds of mutual and voluntary separation without cohabitation for six months, or separation (voluntary or otherwise) without cohabitation for one year.

If you live in Maryland or Virginia, you can get a divorce on the grounds of adultery, desertion, imprisonment, and voluntary separation without cohabitation for one year (six months in Virginia if you do not have minor children and you and your spouse have entered into a property settlement agreement). Virginia also has added cruelty as well as sodomy (oral sex) and buggery (anal sex) committed outside your marriage as grounds, and Maryland has insanity on its list.

Also in Maryland and Virginia, you can file for divorce under more than one ground; for instance, adultery and desertion.

Waiting Periods for Absolute Divorce	Adultery (MD, VA)	No specified waiting period, if residency requirement has been fulfilled.
	Cruelty (VA)	One year of separation for such act.
	Desertion (MD, VA)	One year.
	Imprisonment (MD, VA)	See Crime.
	Voluntary Separation	One year: Virginia and Maryland; six months: District of Columbia.
	Insanity (MD)	Three years.
	Sodomy, Buggery (VA)	No specified waiting period, if residency requirement has been fulfilled.
	Nonvoluntary Separation	One year: District of Columbia and Virginia; two years: Maryland.

Adultery (MD, VA)

Adultery is sexual intercourse between a married person and someone other than the spouse. In Maryland, neither cunnilingus nor fellatio, which the law defines as sodomy, is a ground for divorce and generally neither is considered adultery. In Virginia, not only is sodomy a ground for divorce, but the ever-protective legislators added buggery as a ground. Buggery is anal intercourse.

How to Prove Adultery

There probably is no such thing as a pleasant adultery case, since names, dates, places, paramours, and the like have to be brought out in the open. If your spouse no longer cares about what you know and is open about the affair, you're lucky. You can then catch your spouse *flagrante delicto,* which means you have your spouse in the flagrant wrong and may not have to worry about hiring detectives,

11

although you may still need one to prove your case in court.

Most adultery cases are proved by circumstantial evidence, which means that you have to establish that your spouse had the disposition and opportunity to commit adultery. As a Virginia case says, "Proof must be strict, satisfactory, and conclusive." Even though it might take a flashcube-popping detective, you should be able to prove that your spouse and his or her lover had a sexual interest in each other, sufficient time for them to spend alone together to commit adultery, and, of course, a date and a meeting place.

Public displays of affection, such as hand-holding, kissing, and hugging between the guilty spouse and the paramour are generally sufficient evidence to indicate an adulterous disposition. Opportunity may be proven by showing that your spouse was seen entering the paramour's apartment at 11 P.M. and not coming out until 8 o'clock the following morning and that they were alone.

Naming the Corespondent

The corespondent is the person whom you charge as having committed adultery with your spouse. The corespondent has the right to hire a lawyer and file an answer to your complaint, thereby becoming a defendant along with your spouse. Naming corespondents can get sticky, particularly if you don't have your facts right. You might be damaging the reputation of an innocent person.

The Adulterer

Adulterers are not equal under the blanket of the law. A woman who is found guilty of adultery in Virginia may lose custody of her children and almost assuredly will lose any rights to alimony. Virginia law specifically states that a wife is not entitled to alimony if the divorce was granted because of her own misconduct. This is not necessarily the case in Maryland.

Condonation

If you knew your spouse committed adultery but continued to live and cohabit with him or her, then adultery can't be used as a ground. Once you resume marital relations, after you learned of the adulterous act, the courts feel that you have forgiven, or "condoned", the act. But, if your spouse starts having affairs again, you can then sue on grounds of adultery. Or, if your spouse has had several affairs and you knew of and condoned only one, you may file on adultery regarding the newly discovered affairs.

In Virginia, a divorce will not be granted on the ground of adultery, sodomy, or buggery if the act occurred more than five years before the start of the suit.

Crimes (MD, VA)   If your spouse has been convicted—not simply charged—of a crime, it is a ground for divorce in Maryland and Virginia.

In Maryland, the conviction can be for either a misdemeanor or a felony, and the spouse has to serve at least 12 months of a minimum three-year sentence in a penitentiary or penal institution.

In Virginia, conviction for a felony and sentence and confinement for one year is all that's necessary to sue on this ground, provided you didn't have sexual relations after the sentencing.

Cruelty (VA)   Cruelty as a ground for divorce is anything that tends to bodily harm and renders cohabitation unsafe or involves danger to life, limb, or health. Angry words, abusive language, humiliating insults, and all malicious annoyances that endanger life or health may constitute the ground of cruelty. Also, cruelty is cumulative and generally consists of successive acts of ill treatment. Because of its cumulative nature, it may be condoned or forgiven up to a certain point, but that will not bar the right to use it as a ground at a later time.

Proof of Cruelty   Most lawyers and judges use the rule of thumb: if you have to ask if it's bad enough to justify your leaving, it isn't.

Desertion and Abandonment (MD, VA)   For all practical purposes, desertion and abandonment are one and the same. There are two elements that have to be present in order to constitute desertion: the willful desire or the intent to desert and the cutting off of sexual relations without good cause. (Nightly "I'm too tired's" or "I'm not in the mood's" are not good reasons.) In Maryland, the abandonment has to continue for 12 uninterrupted months, must be deliberate and final, and beyond any reasonable expectation of reconciliation. There are also two types of desertion—actual desertion and constructive desertion. Both require a continuous separation for at least one year before you file for a divorce.

13

Actual Desertion	When your spouse packs bags, books, and toothpaste, walks out the door, moves into another apartment, and stays there, he or she is guilty of actual desertion. The spouse voluntarily leaves and has no plans to return except perhaps to pick up a forgotten belonging.
Constructive Desertion	You also can be deserted even if your spouse doesn't leave. If your spouse's behavior is so cruel or despicable that you find yourself dialing suicide prevention, you can leave and charge your spouse with constructive desertion. As a Virginia case law states, "Cruelty on the part of the husband which results in the wife's enforced separation from bed and board is tantamount to desertion on his part." (This is also true of wives.) The problem is defining marital misconduct. Often sad but true, nagging, bickering, and jealousy do not always justify leaving. The following are some cases of marital misconduct that have been applied to constructive desertion:

• Willful refusal of sex, without just cause and nonperformance of other marital duties as to practically destroy the homelife.

• Conduct that endangers a spouse's life, safety, health, and even self-respect (although an isolated assault or two will not necessarily constitute cruelty unless the act was particularly severe and atrocious).

• One spouse's failure to move if, for example, the other gets a job transfer. The exception is if one spouse's choice of domicile is unsafe or unsuitable for the other.

• In Virginia, if a husband is able to afford a home separate and apart from his parents and relatives but fails to do so.

If the Deserter Returns	Your spouse has left you, spent six months chasing butterflies, and suddenly wakes up one morning and decides that you're the one after all. In good faith, your spouse shows up at your doorstep and begs you to forgive and forget. If you say yes, then all is well. But if you say no and refuse to even see or listen to your spouse, then, strange but true, your spouse could sue you for desertion. The waiting period would start all over again beginning with the time of your refusal. Keep in mind that "good faith" is the key. If, for example, your husband deserted you and then tried to return only after realizing what the high costs of his alimony and legal fees would be, his desire to return would not necessarily be considered as being in "good faith."

Insanity (MD)	Your spouse must be judged permanently and incurably insane and, in Maryland, be confined in an institution or a hospital for a minimum of three years. To prove insanity, two or more psychiatrists are needed to testify that your spouse is incurable and that there is no hope of recovery. The court will appoint an attorney to act in the defense of the person purported to be insane, the costs of which are usually borne by the plaintiff.
Voluntary Separation (DC, MD, VA)	The closest the District of Columbia, Maryland, and Virginia come to a "no fault" divorce is what is known as voluntary separation from bed and board without cohabitation. It usually means that you and your spouse have separated after mutually and voluntarily agreeing that you no longer wish to live together as husband and wife and that there's no hope for a reconciliation. Your spouse can't threaten or blackmail you into leaving; you separate because you both want to. To get a divorce on this ground you have to be separated for one year in Maryland and Virginia; six months in the District of Columbia.

If your spouse wants a separation and you don't, it's still possible to file under this ground, but the wait is longer. In the District of Columbia and Virginia, it takes one year of living apart, while Maryland requires two years. In Virginia, to obtain a divorce based upon grounds of living separate and apart, one spouse must have vocalized an intent to terminate the marriage. That intent must be proven to have existed at the time the one year clock begins to tick and must be attested to by at least one independent witness.

Whether the separation is voluntary or not so voluntary, it has to be continuous. This does not mean that you and your spouse can't meet for lunch or dinner on occasion, but it does mean that you can't have sexual relations with each other. If a candlelight dinner intended to discuss your children's report cards ends up kindling your sexual desire for each other, and you follow your passions into bed, then your waiting period has to start all over again. It will begin the day after your bedroom encounter even if you've been on good behavior for 11½ months. Sex between you and your spouse is strictly forbidden during your waiting period. Sex with others can be a problem too; the grounds for your divorce could change.

In a Maryland case a couple mutually agreed to separate. Mrs. O. found a new boy friend and everything was rosy until Mr. O. asked her to share their attorney's expenses. She refused. So Mr. O. hired a detective who spent the night watching the boy friend arriving but not leaving until the following morning. Mr. O. charged adultery. He won.

Most lawyers prefer the voluntary separation cases and try to get their clients to "come around." There are two reasons lawyers prefer voluntary separation as a ground. One, it is easy to prove. All that's generally needed is the testimony of the plaintiff and the plaintiff's witness that the separation in fact occurred. Two, it's a nice clean ground. There's no guilt attached and there's no dirty laundry in court. Remember that divorce proceedings are public record and can be read by anyone any time the court clerk's office is open. Also, this kind of case could save attorneys' fees because there is less time involved.

In the District of Columbia and Virginia, it isn't absolutely necessary for the couple to live under separate roofs even though they file for voluntary separation. A D.C. ruling noted that "the essential thing is not separate roofs but separate lives so as to abandon with apparent permanency of intention the relation of husband and wife." One couple was granted a divorce even though they continued to live in the same house but did not sleep or eat together. Another couple missed out because, although they continued to live in the same house and didn't eat or sleep together, they continued to represent themselves to others as being married. Their desire to keep up appearances cost them their divorce.

In Virginia, if you and your spouse choose to remain under one roof while living separate and apart, you will want at least one independent witness (a very frequent visitor may suffice) to testify as to your living separate and apart with no cohabitation for the period of one year (or six months, if applicable).

Grounds for Annulment
In the District of Columbia, Maryland, and Virginia, there are two types of annulment. In the first type, the marriage is declared void *ab initio,* or from its inception, as though it had never existed. You don't legally have to go to court to have the marriage declared void *ab initio,* although it's a good idea to. The second type is called voidable—you actually have to go to court and have it declared void.

In the District of Columbia, a marriage can be annulled on the grounds of bigamy; when the marriage was contracted during the insanity of either party, unless there was voluntary cohabitation after the insanity was discovered; when the marriage was procured by fraud or coercion; when either party was matrimonially incapacitated at the time of marriage without the knowledge of the other and continued to be so incapacitated (such as impotency); when either party was not of legal consent age (unless there was voluntary cohabitation after obtaining the age of legal consent), but the suit must be filed by the party who hadn't obtained legal consent age.

Annulment is also available in Maryland, and in some cases it can be obtained under the name of a divorce. An annulment can be obtained *ab initio* for bigamy and for lacking age of consent, and a marriage can be declared void if the parties didn't really intend to marry or where they are incapacitated, as in insanity, intoxication, fraud, and duress.

In Virginia, the grounds for annulment of marriage are bigamy; impotency at the time of marriage; conviction of a felony prior to marriage but not known until after the "I do's"; the wife's pregnancy at the time of the marriage with someone else's child—a fact unknown to her husband; the husband's siring of a child by another woman within ten months after the marriage; or either party's having been (without the knowledge of the other) a prostitute before the marriage. If either party lacks capacity to consent to the marriage because of mental incapacity or infirmity, or if either party is under the age of consent, the marriage may be declared void by the court.

Also, any marriage that is expressly prohibited by statute in either the District of Columbia, Maryland, or Virginia, is voidable by annulment.

Grounds for Legal Separation

Many people who, for personal or religious reasons, do not wish to obtain a full divorce can get a legal separation or "limited divorce" instead. Legal separations are very much like divorce with the major difference being that the parties cannot remarry. You are, in effect, still legally married at the same time that you are legally separated.

In order to obtain a legal separation, you must meet residency requirements, grounds, and other legally prescribed laws just as you have to in a case for absolute divorce. Legal separations also can involve property settlements, alimony, and child support and custody.

In the District of Columbia, it is called "legal separa-

17

tion from bed and board" and the grounds are mutual and voluntary separation for six months without cohabitation; separation without cohabitation for one year; adultery; and cruelty.

Maryland calls it a "divorce a mensa et thoro" (Latin for from table and bed). The grounds for obtaining a limited divorce in Maryland are cruelty; excessively vicious conduct; abandonment and desertion; and voluntarily living separate and apart without cohabitation and any expectation of reconciliation.

The Maryland courts also may grant a limited divorce even though you are seeking an absolute divorce. The courts also may decree these divorces forever or for a limited time only. And finally, Maryland's divorces a *mensa et thoro* may be revoked by the courts at any time upon the joint applications of the parties to be discharged. In such cases, you return to the state of being legally married.

In Virginia, a legal separation also is called a "divorce from bed and board" and may be granted under the grounds of cruelty; reasonable apprehension of bodily hurt; and willful desertion or abandonment.

Proving Grounds For Legal Separation

In order to prove the grounds for legal separation, you must go through the same processes of proof as you would in a case for an absolute divorce. The courts do not take legal separations any lighter than they do divorce.

Residency

Divorce laws apply only to the residents of a state, and each state has its own residency requirements. In Maryland the residency requirement is one year; in Virginia and the District of Columbia it is six months. The law absolutely requires that you be a resident for the stated period of time immediately prior to and at the time that you file for a divorce. You cannot have lived in Virginia for six months before moving to Nebraska for another six months and then come back to Virginia to file for a divorce. However, once you have filed, you can move anywhere in the world. (See Appendix for other states' residency requirements.)

*Same State,
Different
Addresses*

You do not have to remain at the same address to fulfill your residency requirement. You can move anywhere within the state from which you are filing. All of your addresses should appear on your divorce forms, not just your present address.

*Proof of
Residency*

Generally, your residency is substantiated by your corroborating witness. The testimony is all that most courts require to verify residency. But cases have been dismissed and even overturned because of improper proof of residency. To be safe, bring copies of your leases with you in court if you have moved a lot (some Virginia counties may require a sheriff's proof of residency and in all Northern Virginia jurisdictions you may have to provide a valid Virginia driver's license bearing your present address for review by the commissioner or judge.

Resident Versus Nonresident	Thousands of divorce cases have been overturned simply because people have moved to a state for the sole purpose of getting a divorce. The six weeks in Reno trick no longer works, as many hapless people have learned. You must prove that you are not living in a state temporarily in order to get a divorce.
How to Establish Residency	Register to vote. Get a driver's license. Get a job. Open charge accounts. Register your car. Take out a library card. The list is endless. But whatever you do, do not maintain a residence in another state that could imply that you do not intend to remain in the state from which you file.
Domicile	Virginia law requires that you prove you are a "domiciliary" as well as a resident of the state. This means that you live in Virginia with the intent to remain there.
County Jurisdiction: Maryland and Virginia	Maryland and Virginia have counties that govern which court your divorce will take place in. This is called venue. In Virginia, you can file suit in the county where you last lived together as husband and wife, in the county where the defendant resides if he or she is still a resident of the state, or in the county where you reside if the defendant is a nonresident. For example, if you lived as husband and wife in Roanoke County and you then moved to Arlington County, while your spouse moved to Ohio, you could file suit in Roanoke County or Arlington County. If your spouse, however, moved to Fairfax County, you could file in either Fairfax County or Roanoke County. You must be careful that you file in the appropriate county or the court may dismiss your suit.

In Maryland, you can file in any county if the defendant is agreeable to filing in a nonresident county. This can have some advantages, since court costs may be less in one county than in another, and the court docket may be shorter, which means you can get the divorce quicker.

Separation Agreements

The separation agreement, which is also known as the property settlement agreement, is simply a written contract dividing your worldly goods, as well as often settling problems such as alimony and custody. It's usually a good idea to have one, although it will add $250 and up to your divorce bill. If you have considerable property as well as children, a lawyer not only will be an absolute necessity but may be your best friend as well. Even if you don't have a lot of possessions, a property settlement agreement often can be the only assurance that you won't be eating cottage cheese with plastic forks for the rest of your life.

Ideally, a property settlement agreement should be worked out when your emotions cool down and you can look at your spouse, car, and silverware with more detachment than anger. That's the ideal, which all too often isn't the case, thus the necessity for a cool, controlled lawyer. Keep in mind that an agreement spells out your legal rights without taking any formal action in a court of law. The agreement may be drawn before or after you have filed suit.

What to Include

The property settlement agreement spells out your marital rights, including the right to alimony, custody of children, child support, ownership of motor vehicles, division

21

of personal property and household goods, division of any real property such as the family ,home or your weekend retreat, medical expenses, whether joint tax returns are to be filed, how and if charge accounts and credit are to be handled, payment of any outstanding bills, provisions for life insurance in the event of the death of the spouse who is providing spousal and child support, division of jointly held stocks or bonds, the division of any checking or savings accounts, who gets to keep the family dog or cat, rights to visit with the children, and any other matter that is in your best interest to put in writing. Whether you actually need a separation agreement is something that only you and your lawyer can determine. But it could save a lot of pain and aggravation to have everything in writing, in the event that there are any misunderstandings at a later point and time.

An Agreement or a Contract?

Your property settlement agreement is both an agreement and a contract. One thing you must be aware of is that it is a legal document that will bind you throughout the years and determine your rights, obligations, and responsibilities deriving from your marriage. A separation agreement is enforceable in a court of law or in the equity branch of the court. If your spouse violates the agreement, you can go into court to seek a judgment for money damages for the violation of the contract. Or, you may go into a court of equity and seek enforcement under the court's equitable powers by requesting your aberrant spouse be held in contempt of court, which can result in a jail sentence, imposed or suspended, a fine or both. Because it is a legal document, it would be wise to hire a lawyer, who would represent your best interests. If your spouse has hired an attorney, you'd be smart to follow suit.

Breaking the Agreement

No contract is necessarily absolute; if you and your spouse want a change in the agreement, it's a simple matter to draw up an addendum, which modifies the original agreement. But the agreement itself cannot be broken without the consent of you and your spouse or by an order of the court. Taking your case to court doesn't necessarily mean that the changes you want will be incorporated. A great deal depends on the way in which the original agreement was written and whether or not the agreement has been brought within the divorce court's jurisdiction.

If the parties have entered into an agreement in

which they specifically state that the agreement is not subject to any court modification, then a court cannot modify that agreement with respect to property rights between the husband and wife. But the court can always modify provisions in an agreement regarding the care, custody, education, or maintenance of any minor children, as well as any provisions specifically left open to the court's review and modification.

What to Include in Your Separation Agreement

As with any agreement, the more you have in writing the better off you will be the long run. The following questions often are settled in separation/property agreements:

Spousal Support/Alimony—Should there be alimony or is one spouse waiving the right to claim alimony, and if so, what is he or she receiving instead? Is a waiver of alimony based on some valid consideration or is it there because a spouse is not entitled to any? Is it modifiable by a court or is it fixed in legal concrete by the language of the agreement? How is it to be paid? Is it a lump sum payment or spaced out over a period of time? Is it to be monthly or weekly? Is one spouse to continue to receive support in the event of remarriage? If so, how much? Is there to be a sliding scale provision for a cost of living increase in the amount of payments, or coupled with the earning ability of either of the spouses? If the paying party gets a raise, does the support payment increase? If the party receiving support gets a raise, do the payments decrease?

Child Support—How much is to be paid for each child? Do the payments terminate at a certain point and time, for example when the child reaches 18 or 21? Or do the child-support payments continue while the child is still in college? Or even in some postgraduate type of school? What is to be the tax treatment of the child support? There are ways of drafting the separation agreement in which the child support can be treated from a tax standpoint in the same manner as alimony is treated. That is, it can be deductible by the husband in his gross income and inclusive in the gross income of the wife. Are there to be additional payments in the event of emergencies: medical, dental and surgical expenses; hospitalization? If so, who is to pay? Is it to be split in half? Are the payments to be set or should they escalate along with the cost of living or consumer price index?

Visitation Rights—What type of rights does the

23

spouse who doesn't have custody have? Is it visitation at any time with reasonable notice to the other party? Or is it on a specific day from one certain hour to another? Who has the right to have the children at holidays and vacations? How many weeks will the noncustodial parent have the children during vacation? Is the vacation to be two weeks at the beginning of the summer or one week at the beginning and one week at the end of the summer? Or is it to be longer? How many times during the week is your spouse entitled to take the children out? Which parent makes decisions regarding the children's education (choice of schools), health (choice of doctors), summer plans (trips, camps), and general welfare? Is the other parent to be consulted? Which parent has final say? May the children be removed from the place where they are to reside? What happens if the custodial parent remarries and wants to move out of the state? If the wife remarries and she has custody, are the children to continue to bear the husband's name?

Medical and Dental Expenses—Is the noncustodial parent to pay medical and dental expenses for the spouse and children in addition to payments of support? What about health insurance? Is it to be a separate expense? How about orthodontic work? What right does the paying spouse have to be consulted with respect to which doctors or dentists are used? Is the payee to check with the payor before the selection of a doctor or dentist is made and the bills are incurred?

Life Insurance—Are there to be provisions for life insurance for the supported spouse in the event that the other spouse dies and there is no provision for the continuance of the alimony payments from the estate? The same thing holds true with respect to child support. Should there be provisions in the agreement for the supporting spouse to maintain a life insurance policy with the children as beneficiaries? When do these benefits terminate?

Children's Education—Who pays for the college expense for the minor children? Does this include the tuition? Does this include the room and board? If room and board are included, does the custodial parent or spouse continue to receive support payments? How about books and transportation allowance to and from school? And how many times is that transportation allowance to be used? At the beginning and end of the semester? During semester breaks, vacation times, and the like? How about an allowance for the children while they are in college? Or for that matter, while they are in high school? Is one spouse to foot the bill for summer camp, piano or ballet lessons, or for a tutor?

Types of Property

There are two types of property. One type of property is real property, which is real estate. The other type is personal property, such as securities, bonds, bank accounts, automobiles, household furniture, jewelry, paintings, books, record collections, and the family dog, to mention a few.

Real Property

Real property includes all real estate. It includes your home, beach house, condominium, or that interest in some real estate investment held in both your names, or titled solely in one spouse's name or held by another for your benefit.

Take an easy piece of real estate, such as the family home. There are several things you can do with the house in the separation agreement. The first is for one spouse to sign over to the other his or her entire interest in the home. (Beware that the language used in a separation or property settlement agreement relative to the terms of the transfer may result in an adverse tax consequence to the transferor.) There's also the possibility of the sale of the property, with an equal division of the proceeds from the sale.

Another practice often followed is giving the right to one of the parties (usually the custodial parent) to remain in the home for a certain period of time, particularly until the children reach their age of majority or become self-supporting. The parties may agree to then sell the property and divide the proceeds from the sale. Another possibility is to allow one party to remain in the home, to have the house appraised, to fix the equities of the parties as of that date, then to allocate whatever appreciation may be attributable to the house to the party who then continues to make the payments, and that person gets whatever increase or decrease in value there may be at the time that the house is actually sold. There are other questions too. If one of the parties remains in the house and that person makes the payments on the house, does that person also get the tax advantages, which include the interest payments and state property taxes as a deduction on his/her income tax return? Or does the other spouse, who is perhaps paying support as well as house payments, have the benefit of that deduction?

With any real estate, similar agreements or trade-offs of interest in properties can be made. For instance, a husband could sign over the family home to the wife in exchange for the wife's signing over to him the beach property and her interest in his share of their investment in their real estate syndicate. Or the wife could sign all properties, other than the family home, over to the husband in exchange for the husband's paying a greater sum in support. Or the husband could pay a lump sum to the wife in exchange for her signing over her interest in any real estate to him.

Often, one spouse desires to purchase the other's interest in joint real estate. You may wish to hire an independent appraiser to determine the fair market value of the property before you and your spouse decide on any "buy out" terms. Again, you can not be overly cautious in considering tax consequences. Be sure to check with your tax accountant before any "buy out" between you and your spouse.

Personal Property

Personal property includes items such as securities, bonds, savings accounts, checking accounts, automobiles, household furniture, jewelry, books, record collections, paintings, and/or other objects of art. Any of these items can be used as a trade-off for other items. A separation agreement should definitely contain some provision as to what should be done with all these accumulated goods.

Discharge of Outstanding Bills and Promise Against Further Pledge of Credit

One of the greatest problems in divorce cases is who pays what. In most contested divorce cases, the real fight is not over the divorce, but over money. All separation agreements should spell out who will pay outstanding bills and up to what point the spouse will pay bills that have been incurred by the other spouse, along with a promise not to utilize the other spouse's credit. The agreement should list precisely which bills one spouse is undertaking to pay and which bills the other will pay, or should state that anything not set out as being the specific obligation of one party will be the other spouse's obligation. This clause should always include terms which will protect one spouse from claims made against the other. In the event bills are not paid as agreed upon an indemnification proviso protects the party acknowledged free of liability.

Attorney's Fees and Court Costs	Every separation agreement should indicate that each of the parties has had independent advice of counsel in the negotiation and preparation of the agreement. It should also contain a provision on who pays the attorney's fees and court costs when the time comes to file for divorce. Again, there are a number of possible ways in which attorney's fees can be handled. Each party can pay his/her own, or one spouse can pay a portion, if not all, of the other's attorney's fees. Finally, there should be a provision covering who should pay legal and court costs for the preparation of any documents necessary to enforce the agreement.
Joint Tax Returns	Another essential ingredient in the separation agreement is a provision for tax returns. It may be advantageous to one spouse to file a joint tax return until the divorce, after which both parties have to file separately. Also, a provision should be included that spells out the obligation of the other spouse to file a joint tax return if requested to do so. The agreement could also cover who will pay any additional taxes as a result of the joint filing, what is to be done with refund checks, and an indemnification clause that holds the other party harmless against any liability for his/her own proportionate share of the tax.
Jewish Divorce	If you are Jewish, you will want to include a provision for a Jewish divorce, or *Get,* as well as a provision as to who shall pay for the cost of it.
Incorporating the Agreement	There are two things that you can do with your property settlement agreement: you can stash it in a drawer somewhere or you can incorporate it into your final divorce decree. If incorporated into the decree, it becomes a court order and is enforceable by the court's contempt powers. If you don't incorporate it into the decree, it simply becomes a contract between you and your spouse, which you would later have to sue upon in a separate action to enforce.
Mutual Releases	Your separation agreement should contain a provision that mutually releases all rights that you may have with one another, except the ground for divorce. Some of the rights that you are waiving are the following: all the right, title, interest, and claim that you might have or may later have as the husband, wife, widower, widow, or next of kin, successor, in and to any real or personal property you now

own or may later acquire; or to participate in any way as executor of your spouse's estate. This portion of the separation agreement should also guarantee that you and your spouse will executive any documents, such as an automobile transfer of title, that may be necessary to effect any part of the separation agreement.

The items listed above are those that you may find in a separation agreement. The list is not intended to be all-inclusive. Every case presents different questions and must be dealt with accordingly. Your separation agreement is also an agreement between you and your spouse to live separate and apart, which is formalized in a written document. This can become quite critical at a later date when you file for your divorce. Therefore, be sure that you are represented by counsel when you enter into your separation agreement.

Sample Separation Agreements   The following are three sample separation agreements. The first does not include property and is often used for people who have divied up everything between themselves. The second property settlement agreement is typical of people who have some—but not a lot of—property, and the third agreement is for people with children and considerable property. It also spells out rights to alimony, insurance, and the like.

(Example 1)   SEPARATION AGREEMENT

THIS AGREEMENT made this ___ day of _____ , 19__ , by and between SAM SPOUSE, residing at 6900 Darren Lane, N.W., Washington, D.C., hereinafter referred to as "Husband," and SARA SPOUSE, residing at 1243 Bradford Road, Bethesda, Maryland, hereinafter referred to as "Wife."

WITNESSETH:
WHEREAS, the parties hereto were married on March 15, 1974, in Southbury, Connecticut, and
WHEREAS, in consequence of disputes and unhappy differences which have arisen between the parties hereto, the said parties have voluntarily and mutually agreed to live separate and apart, and are now and since the 18th day of September, 1983, living separate and apart.
NOW, THEREFORE, in consideration of the premises

and the mutual promises and undertakings herein contained, and other good and valuable considerations, receipt of which is hereby acknowledged, the parties voluntarily and mutually covenant and agree as follows:

1. The parties may and shall at all times hereafter live and continue to live separate and apart. Each shall be free from interference, authority and control, direct or indirect, by the other as fully as if he or she were sole and unmarried. Each may reside at such place or places as he or she may select. Each may, for his or her separate use and benefit, conduct, carry on, and engage in any business, profession or employment which to him or her may seem advisable. Each shall be at liberty to act and do as he or she sees fit, and to conduct his or her personal and social life as freely and as fully as if he or she were sole and unmarried.

2. The parties shall not annoy, molest or otherwise interfere with each other, nor shall either of them compel or attempt to compel the other to cohabit with him or her, by any means whatever.

3. The parties further agree that the execution of this document shall in no way be considered or construed as a waiver of or bar to any cause for divorce which either of the parties may now have against the other or which may hereafter accrue, or be considered or construed as constituting a ground or cause for divorce.

4. This agreement contains the entire understanding of the parties. There are no representations, warranties, promises, covenants or understandings other than those expressly set forth herein.

5. Each party hereto declares that he or she fully understands the facts and all his or her legal rights and liabilities; and that each believes the agreement to be fair, just and reasonable, and that each signs the agreement freely and voluntarily.

IN WITNESS WHEREOF, the parties hereto have set their hands and seals to two counterparts of this agreement, each of which will constitute an original, this ___ day of _____, 19__.

Witness:

_____   _____ (SEAL)

as to Husband   SAM SPOUSE

_____   _____ (SEAL)

as to Wife   SARA SPOUSE

DISTRICT OF COLUMBIA   :
                        : ss.
CITY OF WASHINGTON   :

On this ___ day of _____, 19__, before me, a Notary Public in and for the District of Columbia, City of Washington aforesaid, personally appeared SAM SPOUSE, personally known or made known to me to be the Husband who executed the foregoing instrument, and made oath under the penalties of perjury that the facts and statements contained in this document are true and that he acknowledged to me that he freely and voluntarily executed the same for the purposes named therein.

WITNESS my hand and seal.

_____
Notary Public

My Commission Expires: _____

STATE OF MARYLAND   :
                        : ss.
COUNTY OF MONTGOMERY   :

On this ___ day of _____, 19__, before me, a Notary Public in and for the State and County aforesaid, personally appeared SARA SPOUSE, personally known or made known to me to be the Wife who executed the foregoing instrument, and made oath under the penalties of perjury that the facts and statements contained in this document are true and that she acknowledged to me that she freely and voluntarily executed the same for the purposes named therein.

WITNESS my hand and seal.

_____
Notary Public

My Commission Expires: _____

(Example 2) PROPERTY SETTLEMENT AGREEMENT

THIS AGREEMENT is made as of the ___ day of _____, 19__, by and between Sara Spouse (hereinafter referred to as the "Wife") and Sam Spouse (hereinafter referred to as the "Husband").

RECITALS

A. The parties to this Agreement were married on June 2, 1978, in Woodbury, Connecticut, and are now Husband and Wife.

B. No children were born as issue of this marriage.

C. As a result of disputes and differences arising between the parties, they separated on June 2, 1982, and have thereafter lived separate and apart.

D. The parties desire hereby to conclude settlement of all questions relating to their property rights; to the maintenance and support of each of the parties by the other; and to all other rights, claims, relationships or obligations between them arising out of their marriage or otherwise.

NOW THEREFORE, in consideration of the mutual promises herein made and of the acts to be performed by the respective parties hereto, it is agreed as follows:

SEPARATION

The parties separated on June 2, 1982, and have continued to live separate and apart. Neither shall molest nor interfere with the other nor attempt to compel the other to cohabit or dwell with him or her.

PERSONAL PROPERTY

1. The parties jointly own certain items of family use personal property. They have agreed to a division of that property and attached hereto as Exhibit One is a list of that property and the division of same exemplified by the parties' initials by each item of property.

2. The parties jointly own the following items of personal property: Dreyfus Liquid Assets Fund—$7,600; one hundred shares of Excalibur Technologies, Inc; Government Investor's Trust—$5,000; State of Maryland Employees Credit Union—$800.00; T. Rowe Price Municipal Bond Fund—$150.00; United States Savings Bonds —$250.00; and a joint savings account at Perpetual American Bank containing approximately $2,000.00. Upon execution of this Agreement, the parties shall equally divide the aforegoing items of personal property; except that the joint savings account at Perpetual American Bank shall be used to pay joint debts of the parties as hereinafter provided in paragraph III.

3. The Wife owns in her name only, a 1980 BMW 2002 automobile, and the Husband owns in his own name only, a 1980 BMW 320i automobile. Each party shall retain his or her respective vehicle free of any claim by the other and the Husband shall be exclusively liable for the outstanding loan on his vehicle held by General Motors Credit Corporation and save the Wife harmless for same.

4. After the division of personal property provided

herein, neither party shall make claim to any item of personal property then in the possession of the other.

REAL PROPERTY

1. The parties own a home as tenants by the entirety known as 666 Gildenhorn Drive, Silver Spring, Montgomery County, Maryland, in which the wife presently resides. The Wife shall have the exclusive right of occupancy of the subject home until November 30, 1985. During the period that the Wife has exclusive occupancy of the subject home, the Wife shall be responsible for all mortgage payments, taxes, insurance, and general upkeep. All major improvements defined as expenses over $150.00 shall be divided equally between the parties. The Wife shall have the exclusive right to deduct all interest and taxes in connection with said home on her federal and state income tax returns during the period of her exclusive occupancy.

2. Prior to November 30, 1985, the Wife shall purchase the Husband's right, title and interest in and to the parties' home. In the event that the Wife shall fail to purchase the Husband's interest by November 30, 1985, the Husband shall purchase the Wife's right, title and interest in and to the parties' home. The consideration to be paid by either party to the other shall be fifty per cent (50%) of the difference between the subject home's market value less the amount of any outstanding liens or mortgages against the property. In determining the market value of the subject home, the Wife shall promptly obtain an appraisal from a certified real estate appraiser at Husband's expense. If the appraisal is unacceptable to the Husband, he shall obtain his own appraisal from a certified real estate appraiser at his expense. The market value shall then be an average of the two (2) appraisals. If the Wife purchases the Husband's equity, she shall be credited for all mortgage payments, principal, interest, taxes and insurance, she makes from June 1, 1984 until November 30, 1985, against the Husband's equity. In addition, she shall receive credit for one-half (1/2) of sale expenses which would occur if the parties sold the subject property to a third party (broker's commission, settlement costs, etc) in the amount of four per cent (4%) of the fair market value. The purchasing party shall receive from the selling party an appropriate deed. All expenses in connection with the property transfer shall be borne by the purchasing party. After transfer, the purchasing party shall save

the selling party harmless for any expenses in connection with the said home including any mortgage, interest, and/or taxes.

DEBTS AND PLEDGES OF CREDIT

Each party convenants that neither he nor she has incurred any debts or obligations heretofore for which the other may be held liable. The parties agree that neither will incur hereafter any liability or obligation whatsoever upon the credit of the other, or for which the other might be held liable. Each party agrees to indemnify and hold harmless the other from any obligation or liability incurred by the other by virtue of a breach of this paragraph.

INSURANCE

The Husband shall maintain the Wife on his policy of hospitalization insurance until such time as a decree of divorce a vinculo matrimonii entered between the parties. Likewise, the Husband shall retain the Wife as the irrevocable beneficiary on all his life insurance policies until such time as either party remarries.

TAXES

The parties shall file joint federal and state income tax returns for the year 1984. In the event of any tax refund or additional taxation, the parties shall divide the refund or additional tax equally (50 – 50).

LIVING EXPENSES

The parties shall equally divide all outstanding bills for ordinary living expenses incurred by the parties up until the date of June 2, 1984 not to exceed the sum of $1,000.00 per person. Husband and Wife shall be responsible for all of their extraordinary personal expenses incurred prior to or subsequent to June 2, 1984.

ATTORNEY'S FEES

The Husband shall pay to the Wife as a contribution toward her attorney's fees for purposes of obtaining a decree of divorce *a Vinculo matrimonii* between the parties, a sum not to exceed $200.00 (two hundred dollars).

RELEASE AND WAIVER

1. Except as otherwise provided for herein, each of the parties hereto shall have and enjoy independently of any claim or right of the other party, all items of real and personal property, of any kind or nature, now or hereafter belonging to him or her and now or hereafter in his or her possession, with full power to dispose of the same as fully and effectually as though he or she were unmarried.

2. That until such time that a decree of divorce *a vinculo matrimonii* is entered between the parties neither party will revise, revoke, amend, nor add codicils to their existing Last Wills & Testaments.

INCORPORATION IN DECREE OF DIVORCE

Nothing herein contained shall be deemed to prevent either of the parties hereto from maintaining a suit for either limited or absolute divorce against the other in any jurisdiction, nor to bar the other from defending against any such suit. In the event any action is instituted, this Agreement shall be presented to the court for its ratification, approval and incorporation, but this Agreement shall not be merged in the decree of any court, and shall in all respects survive the same and be forever binding and conclusive upon the parties.

MISCELLANEOUS PROVISIONS

1. A modification, waiver or novation of any of the provisions of this Agreement shall be effective only if made in writing and executed with the same formality as this Agreement. The failure of either party to insist upon strict performance of any of the provisions of this Agreement shall not be construed as a waiver of any subsequent default of the same or different nature.

2. Each of the parties hereto shall, from time to time, at the request of the other, execute, acknowledge and deliver to the other party any and all further instruments that may be reasonably required to give full force and effect to the provisions of this Agreement.

3. If any provision of this Agreement is held to be invalid or unenforceable, all of the other provisions shall, nevertheless, continue in full force and effect.

4. This Agreement contains the entire understanding of the parties, and there are no representations, warranties, covenants or undertaking of, by or between he parties other than those expressly set forth herein.

5. Except as otherwise stated herein, all of the provisions of this Agreement shall be binding upon the respective heirs, next of kin, executors and administrators of the parties.

6. This Agreement shall be construed in accordance with the laws of the State of Maryland.

7. Both parties acknowledge that they have had the opportunity to secure the representation of counsel of his or her own choice and that they are aware of both the legal and practical effect of the provisions of this

Agreement, and they both acknowledge that this is a fair Agreement and is not the result of any fraud, duress or undue influence exercised by either party upon the other, or by any other person or persons upon either, and they further agree that this Agreement contains the entire understanding of the parties. There are no representations, promises, warranties, covenants or undertakings other than those expressly set forth herein.

SENATE BILL 604

Except for the right, which each of the parties respectively reserves, to assert as a ground for divorce any cause or ground which either of them might now or hereafter have against the other, and except for the rights provided in this Agreement, the parties for themselves and their respective heirs, personal representatives and assigns, do hereby mutually release, waive, surrender and assign unto the other, his or her heir, personal representatives and assigns, all claims, demands, accounts, and causes of action which either of them may have against the other or against his or her property, or rights, now or hereafter acquired, whether arising out of the marriage or otherwise, including, but not limited to, any claim or claims arising under the marital property act, Chapter 794 (1978) Laws of Maryland, presently codified as Sections 3-6A-02 through 3-6A-07, Courts and Judicial Proceedings Article, Annotated Code of Maryland, as Amended (1980 Cum. Supp.), or any amendments thereto, and any claim against the other or against his or her property now or hereafter acquired, or by virtue of any future change in the residence or domicile of either of the parties, or any future change in the situs of any property of either of the parties, and any claim against either or the other or against his or her property by virtue of any future change of any law of this or any other state or territory subsequent to the execution of this Agreement, concerning marital rights or property rights, whether said change results from legislative enactment or judicial pronouncement

ALIMONY

1. The parties agree that the terms of this Agreement are fair and reasonable. They, therefore, permanently waive any and all claims for alimony or spousal support that either may have had against the other, now or in the future, and accept in lieu thereof the provisions of this Agreement.

IN WITNESS WHEREOF, the parties have set their hands and seals on the date first above written.
WITNESS:

_____   _____(SEAL)

(SARA SPOUSE)

_____   _____(SEAL)

(SAM SPOUSE)

STATE OF MARYLAND   :

TO WIT:

COUNTY OF MONTGOMERY   :

I HEREBY CERTIFY that before the undersigned Notary Public personally appeared Sara Spouse, known to me to be the person whose name is subscribed to the within instrument, who, after being sworn, made oath in due form of law that the matters and facts set forth in the foregoing Agreement with respect to the voluntary separation of the parties are true and correct as therein stated and acknowledged said Agreement to be her act.

WITNESS, my hand and official seal on this ___ day of _____, 198__.

_____

(Notary Public)

My Commission Expires: _____

STATE OF MARYLAND   :

TO WIT:

COUNTY OF MONTGOMERY   :

I HEREBY CERTIFY that before the undersigned Notary Public personally appeared Sam Spouse, known to me to be the person whose name is subscribed to the within instrument, who, after being sworn, made oath in due form of law that the matters and facts set forth in the foregoing Agreement with respect to the voluntary separation of the parties are true and correct as therein stated and acknowledged said Agreement to be his act.

WITNESS, my hand and official seal on this ___ day of _____, 198__.

_____

(Notary Public)

My Commission Expires: _____

EXHIBIT

DINING ROOM
Rug (H)
Table & Chairs (H)
Buffet (H)
Round Table (W)
Pewter Set (H)
Crystal Bowl (W)
Brass Candlesticks (W)
Silver Pitcher (H)
Silver Plate (W)
Lamp (W)
Glass Candlesticks (W)
Table Cloths, etc. (H)

KITCHEN
White Table & Chairs (W)
Brown Dishes (H)
Stainless Silverware (W)
Tiffany Lamp (W)
Other Items (DIVIDED)

BASEMENT
Pine Table & Chairs (W)

PATIO
Lounge Chairs (ONE EACH)
Yellow Web Chair (ONE EACH)
Picnic Set (W)
Grill (W)

DEN
Sofa (H)
Rocker (W)
Coffee Table (H)
Rug (W)
Sony 17" Television (W)
Pictures (W)

GUEST ROOM
Bed (W)
Rocker (W)
Dresser & Mirror (W)
Lamp (H)
Photos & Pictures (W)
Black & White TV (W)

MASTER BEDROOM
Bed & Headboard (H)
Lamp (H)
Dresser (W)
Sony 15" Television (H)

LIVING ROOM
Sofa (W)
Coffee Table (W)
Brown Chairs (W)
End Tables (W)
Egg Lamp (W)
New Stereo Equipment (H)
    Turntable
    Cassette Deck
    Amplifier
    Reel to Reel
    Tape Deck
    Speakers
Old Stereo Equipment (W)
    Turntable
    Amplifier
    Speakers
    Tuner
Plants & Paintings (W)
Cubes (H)
Eames Chair (H)
Lenox Bowl (H)
Crystal Bowl (W)
Ship's Decanter (W)
Crystal Glasses (W)
Crystal Vase (H)
Crystal Teapot (H)
Crystal Pitcher (W)
Boda Vase (H)
Jane's Vase (H)
Overhead Lamp (W)

MISCELLANEOUS
Ray Heetner's Rug (W)
Orange BMW (H)
White BMW (W)

*H = Husband
 W = Wife

(Example 3)
SEPARATION AND PROPERTY SETTLEMENT AGREEMENT

THIS AGREEMENT, made and entered into this ___ day of
_____, 19__, by and between SAM SPOUSE, residing at
6900 Darren Lane, N.W., Washington, D.C., hereinafter
referred to as the "Husband," and SARA SPOUSE, residing
at 1243 Bradford Road, Bethesda, Maryland, hereinafter
referred to as the "Wife":

WITNESSETH:

WHEREAS, the parties hereto are husband and wife,
having been lawfully married on October 12, 1971 in
Luray, Virginia, and

WHEREAS, three (3) children were born of the aforesaid marriage, namely, Robert John Spouse, born March
13, 1973; Marilyn Joy Spouse, born June 14, 1974; and Jill
Lorraine Spouse, born on June 22, 1972, and

WHEREAS, in consequence of certain disputes and irreconcilable differences, the parties hereto have mutually and voluntarily agreed to separate and live apart
from each other commencing on the ___ day of _____,
19__, and by reason of which the parties have determined
that such separation will be in the best interests of the
marriage and each of them, and

WHEREAS, the parties hereto are mutually desirous
of entering into this separation and property settlement agreement for the purpose of fixing their personal
and property rights, determining the custody of the
minor children of the parties hereto, and affecting a
full and final settlement between them as to all matters
now existing by reason of their marriage heretofore
solemnized.

NOW, THEREFORE, in consideration of the premises
and the mutual promises, covenants, and agreements
hereinafter contained and acknowledged by the parties
hereto, the parties do mutually and voluntarily agree as
follows:

1. CUSTODY. The wife shall have the full care, custody and control of the minor children of the parties
hereto, namely Robert John, Marilyn Joy, and Jill Lorraine Spouse, subject to the husband's right to see and
visit any and all said children at all reasonable times
and places, including but not limited to one day every
weekend; minimum of two weeks during the summer vacation

period; every other Christmas, beginning December 25, 1984; and any other time that the parties hereto may agree upon or the children may desire to visit with their father. The husband agrees to give the wife advance notice prior to his desire to see and visit the minor children, such notice shall be at least twenty-four (24) hours prior to the time said husband wishes to visit with the children. In order that the husband's rights may not be impaired, the wife shall maintain a residence within a 50 mile radius of Harrisonburg, Virginia. This provision, however, shall not prevent the wife from taking the children on brief trips. The parties also shall confer with each other on all important matters pertaining to the children's health, welfare, education, and upbringing in order to promote the children's best interests in a harmonious fashion. Each party chall promptly notify the other in case of a child's serious illness, which is any illness that confines a child to bed for more than two days. Both the husband and the wife covenant and agree that they will in no manner, directly or indirectly, seek to influence or alienate the minor children against the other.

2. SUPPORT AND MAINTENANCE. The husband shall pay to the wife, as maintenance and support for each of the minor children of the parties hereto, the sum of Fifty Dollars ($50.00) per week, per child, commencing on the 1st Friday following the execution of this agreement and for each and every Friday thereafter, until said child attains his or her twenty-first birthday, death, marriage, or emancipation, whichever occurs first. The wife does hereby covenant and agree that as long as the husband continues to pay the aforegoing payments for the maintenance and support of said children, the husband shall be entitled to claim said minor children as an exemption on his Federal and State income tax returns. In addition, the husband shall pay medical, dental, surgical, nursing, and hospital expenses incurred for the children. The wife shall not make any commitment for such expenses without the husband's written consent, except in the case of emergency. The husband also shall incur the cost of sending the children to college to include tuition fees plus a reasonable living allowance to be agreed upon between the parties. The wife agrees to pay for half the expense of summer camps for the children, with the choice of camps and the amount of expenses subject to mutual agreement.

3. MEDICAL INSURANCE. Notwithstanding the provisions heretofore made for the maintenance and support of the minor children in paragraph two (2) above, the husband covenants and agrees to continue in full force and effect, and to pay for the same, a medical, hospital and surgical insurance plan for the benefit of the wife and children of the parties hereto, until the parties are divorced. Upon the divorce of the parties hereto, the husband shall continue said medical, hospital and surgical insurance for the minor children until each of said children attains his or her twenty-first birthday, death, marriage or emancipation, whichever event occurs first. The husband further agrees to pay for all medical and dental expenses necessarily incurred for the benefit of the wife until the parties are divorced.

4. AUTOMOBILE. The husband does hereby release and relinquish unto the wife, any and all of his rights, title and interest in and to the 1981 Dodge Aries or 1982 Chevrolet Camaro now titled in the name of the husband. The husband further agrees that he will execute all papers necessary to transfer said automobile into the name of the wife. The wife covenants and agrees to maintain and pay for the automobile insurance on said vehicle to be conveyed to her, and she covenants and agrees to save the husband harmless and to indemnify him against any debts or obligations incurred in connection with her operation and ownership of the automobile.

5. HOUSEHOLD FURNITURE. The husband hereby covenants and agrees and transfers unto the wife all his right, title and interest in and to all the household furnishings, furniture, appliances, bric-a-brac, and all other items of personal property and household effects now located in the home, located at 1243 Bradford Road, Bethesda, County of Montgomery, Maryland. The husband shall be entitled to remove all his personal belongings, clothes and certain other items heretofore agreed upon between the parties hereto.

6. LIFE INSURANCE. The husband covenants and agrees to maintain and pay all premiums, as and when they become due, on the life insurance policy in the amount of Seventy Thousand Dollars ($70,000.00), with a provision for double indemnity in the event of accidental death, and to retain the wife as the primary beneficiary thereof until the death of the wife.

7. TAX REFUND. The husband covenants and agrees the wife shall be entitled to the Federal and State tax refund

for calendar year 1984. The husband agrees that he will endorse said tax return checks immediately upon the request of the wife.

8. DEBTS AND FUTURE LIABILITIES. The husband covenants and agrees that he shall be responsible for all debts incurred by either both the husband and wife prior to the date of this agreement and to indemnify and hold the wife harmless from the payment thereof. The parties hereto agree not to hereafter seek any credit in the name of the other and not to make, or cause to be made, any obligation for which the other could be held liable or responsible; and that each of the parties shall hereafter be free to do as he or she sees fit without any obligation to the other.

9. ALIMONY. The husband does hereby covenant and agree to pay unto the wife as alimony for her maintenance and support, the sum of One Hundred Dollars ($100.00) per week, commencing on the 1st Friday after the execution of this agreement, and for each and every Friday thereafter until death of the wife, marriage of the wife, or death of the husband.

10. GENERAL RELEASES.

a) The husband does hereby release and relinquish unto the wife all his right, title and interest in and to any personal property, tangible or intangible, not hereinbefore mentioned held in the name of the wife, and the wife does hereby release and relinquish unto the husband all of her right, title and interest in and to any personal property, tangible or intangible, not hereinbefore mentioned now held in the name of the husband.

b) The parties agree to and do hereby release each other from any statutory share, dower or courtesy interest which they have in and to any property owned by the other party, or which may hereafter be acquired by either party.

c) The parties agree to sign any documents necessary to effect any provisions contained herein and the husband further covenants and agrees that he will provide the wife proof of the payment of the life insurance policy on an annual basis.

11. MUTUAL AND VOLUNTARY SEPARATION. The husband and wife shall and may live separate and apart from each other, and each may reside from time to time at such place or places as she or he may decide or determine, and neither shall be required to live or cohabit with the other. Each shall be free from any interference, restraint, au-

thority and control, direct or indirect, on the part of the other as fully as if he or she were sole and unmarried. Neither shall molest, disturb or trouble the other in any way. Each may engage in any business, profession or employment as may be desired for their separate use and benefit.

12. INCORPORATION AND NONMODIFICATION OF AGREEMENT IN FINAL DECREE. It is the desire of both parties hereto that this agreement, and the entire provisions hereof, be ratified, confirmed and approved by the Court in any action or proceeding now pending, or hereafter commence, in any Court by either party hereto against the other for the dissolution of the bonds of matrimony; That this agreement be incorporated in any Decree or Order entered therein; That said agreement shall not merge therein, and that the terms, conditions and provisions herein contained for support, maintenance, property rights and the personal rights between the husband and wife shall not be subject to any modification whatsoever by any Court. The parties hereto do further agree that each or either of them will present this agreement to the Court and request that it be ratified, confirmed and approved without modification whatsoever and that it be made an enforceable part of any Decree or Order entered therein and the parties hereto further agree that neither of them will oppose such ratification, confirmation or approval, nor shall either of them seek any modification as to support, maintenance, alimony, property rights, custody, personal rights as between the husband and wife.

13. SEVERABILITY AND WAIVER. No waiver of any breach or default hereunder shall be deemed a waiver of any subsequent breach or default. This agreement contains the entire understanding of the parties. If any of the provisions of this agreement are held to be invalid or unenforceable, all other provisions, nonetheless, will and shall remain in full force and effect.

14. VOLUNTARY ACT OF EACH PARTY. Each party hereto acknowledges that he or she is making this agreement of his or her own free will and volition, and acknowledges that no coercion, force, pressure or undue influence has been used against either party in the making of this agreement, either by the other party to this agreement or by any other person or persons. The parties further declare that each has had independent legal advice by counsel of his or her own selection; That each has been fully

apprised as to the full nature and extent of the assets and liabilities of each other and of the legal rights of each, and that after such advice, knowledge and information, each signs this agreement freely and voluntarily, neither relying upon any representations other than those expressly set forth herein. No oral statement or prior written matter extrinsic to this agreement shall have any force or effect.

15. APPLICABLE LAW. This agreement shall be construed under and in accordance with the laws of the State of Maryland.

IN WITNESS WHEREOF, the parties hereunto have set their hands and seals.

Witness:

_____   _____ (SEAL)
                             SAM SPOUSE

_____   _____ (SEAL)
                             SARA SPOUSE

STATE OF MARYLAND   :
                         : SS.
COUNTY OF MONTGOMERY   :

I, the undersigned, a Notary Public in and for the County and State aforesaid, do hereby certify that SAM SPOUSE whose name is signed to the foregoing Separation and Property Settlement Agreement, personally appeared before me and executed the same under the penalty of perjury for the purposes therein contained, and that he did further acknowledge and make oath in due form of law that the matters contained herein are true and that this Agreement was the mutual and voluntary act of the parties hereto.

GIVEN under my hand this ___ day of _____, 19__.

                             _____
                             Notary Public

My Commission Expires: _____

STATE OF MARYLAND   :
                         : SS.
COUNTY OF MONTGOMERY   :

I, the undersigned, a Notary Public in and for the County and State aforesaid, do hereby certify that SARA SPOUSE whose name is signed to the foregoing Separation and Property Settlement Agreement, personally appeared before me and executed the same under the penalty of perjury for the purposes therein contained, and that she did further acknowledge and make oath under due form of law that the matters contained herein are true and that this Agreement was the mutual and voluntary act of each of the parties hereto.

GIVEN under my hand this ___ day of _____, 19__.

_____

                                      Notary Public

My Commission Expires: _____

Property

All marriages involve property, whether it's real property such as your house or your retreat, or it's personal property such as your car or home furnishings. And all actions for divorce lay claim to the answer of "Who gets what?"

Basically, you decide the answer. The courts do not want to get too involved as arbitrator between you and your spouse and your inability to decide who keeps the fish tanks or the living room carpet. However, to make the going a bit easier, the law does step in and lay some ground rules regarding what's yours to keep and what belongs to you and your spouse.

Separate Property

Property that you can do with as you wish, as defined by law, is called "separate property." This is property that is yours to keep regardless of what your spouse says or thinks. It's simply yours. Separate property includes:

(1) All real and personal property acquired by you before the marriage;

(2) All property acquired during the marriage by bequest, devise, descent, survivorship, or by a gift from someone other than your spouse (your spouse's gifts to you are considered "marital property"); and

(3) All property that you acquired during the marriage in exchange for or from the proceeds of sale of separate property, *provided that such property is maintained as separate property.*

If you place your separate property in joint names, or if you use your liquid assets to buy household furnishings, or if you comingle your funds with funds held jointly by you and your spouse, then the court may determine that your generous gestures are marital property and are subject to distribution.

Marital
Property

Aside from separate property, the law also defines what is called "marital property." Marital property belongs to you and your spouse and is that which gets divided, sold, or distributed because of a divorce action. It is not yours to keep; it is yours to share with your spouse. Marital property consists of:

(1) All property titled in the names of you and your spouse; and

(2) All property acquired by either you or your spouse during the course of your marriage, but does not include property defined as separate property.

The division of marital property is often contentious and bitter. Sparks can fly high and hot when it comes to deciding who gets to keep what, whether it's the house, the family pet, or a set of bath towels of which you are both particularly fond.

If you and your spouse reach an impasse over who will get the garden hose, the amplifier, or the Christmas tree ornaments, you most likely will be better off sitting it out until the marital volcano cools, rather than spending your lawyer's time, your money, or the court's time making the determination for you. Your money will be spent more wisely, as will be the court's and your lawyer's time, by concentrating on items of larger value. If you spend your energy trying to wrestle the tea cart from your spouse, you may get it, but your spouse also may end up with the house and a much less expensive legal bill. It would be wise for you to not lose sight of the financial realities over sentimentality and emotionalism. Although it is often difficult to separate the two when faced with a separation or divorce, the wisdom of this caveat is best seen when the bills arrive.

If you cannot decide on how your property is to be divided and your lawyers cannot assist you in this, then you do have the right to let the court make the division for you.

Present laws in the District of Columbia, Maryland, and Virginia provide for an equitable division of property acquired during the marriage. This does not, however, mean a fifty-fifty split.

As the District of Columbia statute succinctly states: The court shall "distribute all other property accumulated during the marriage, regardless of whether title is held individually or by the parties in a form of joint tenancy or tenancy by the entireties, in a manner that is equitable, just and reasonable, after considering all relevant factors including, but not limited to: the duration of the marriage, any prior marriage of either party, the age, health occupation, amount and sources of income, vocational skills, employability, assets, debts, and needs of each of the parties, provisions for the custody of minor children, whether the distribution is in lieu of or in addition to maintenance, and the opportunity of each for future acquisition of assets and income. The court shall also consider each party's contribution to the acquisition, preservation, appreciation, dissipation, or depreciation in value of the assets subject to distribution under this subsection, and each party's contribution as a homemaker or to the family unit."

Virginia and Maryland are very much the same, although Maryland has taken the question of property ownership and use a big step further.

Under Maryland law, the court may not transfer the ownership of personal property from one spouse to the other, but the court may grant a decree which states what the ownership interest of each spouse is as well as order a partition or sale in lieu of partition and a division of the proceeds on any jointly owned property. For example, the court can order you to sell your house—and within a specified period of time—and then have you divide the profits according to how the court decided the split was to be made.

A Maryland court also can reserve the power for 90 days after the final divorce decree to determine which property is marital property and then divide it accordingly, including putting a monetary value on it and ordering one spouse to pay the other for it.

Family Use Personal Property (MD)

The state of Maryland recognizes another type of property called "family use personal property." This includes the family home and everything in it. Family use personal property comes into play when there are children—particularly minor children. The Maryland legislators felt that children should continue to live in the environment and community that is familiar to them, and for that reason, they should be able to stay in the family home with all its contents for a period of up to three years from the date of the divorce decree.

What this means is that a court in Maryland may award the custodial spouse full use of the family home and all of its contents to use for a specified period of time not to exceed three yeras. However, if the custodial spouse remarries, the use and possession authority of the court no longer applies.

Perhaps the biggest bane in this Maryland law is that family use property also can include your separate property. If you owned your home before you married, your home under this provision of the law is not regarded as your personal property until the court specified period for family use is over. You could have to wait up until three years to get your house back.

However, if you owned the home jointly or acquired it after your marriage, the court may deem it marital property and divide the proceeds or value accordingly after the specified period.

Finally, the court may order either or both of the spouses to pay all or any part of any mortgage or rent payments, including maintenance, insurance, assessments and taxes, and other similar expenses regarding the property while it is being used for family use.

This law alone makes it necessary to see an attorney.

Child Support & Custody

Once upon a time, mothers remained mothers in divorce cases and fathers became weekend or Sunday visitors who took their children to the zoo and dutifully returned them "home" to mother at the end of visitation periods. No more. Child custody is no longer the sole province of women; men can—and do—get custody as well. But the woman is still generally considered by most courts to be the natural custodian of children, particularly if the children are young and if she meets the qualifications of "fitness." Most custody cases, however, do not even reach the court stage—custody is usually determined by the parents.

Fit and Proper

Believe it or not, the court—not you—acts as a custodian over your children and even has the right to take them away (declare them adoptable or assign them to a foster home) if both you and your spouse are considered unfit and improper parents. The welfare of the children is paramount as far as the court is concerned. There is no absolute definition of a fit and proper parent, but if you swear and drink a lot, abuse your children, and have various nightly visitors of the opposite sex, you can be fairly sure that the court will not deem you to be fit and proper. All of this has to be proven, however, and hearsay evidence generally doesn't suffice.

49

*Joint
Custody*

A new trend in custody proceedings is the awarding of joint or shared custody to both parents. The philosophical premise behind joint custody is that both parents are responsible for the decisions and care of the children. It is a way to allow both parents input into the major decisions affecting the children's life. That's all very nice and apple pie sounding, but too often doesn't work and, in fact, is not one of the court's favorite ways of working things out. As an Illinois court ruled, "Joint custody is usually an unworkable arrangement." And a Vermont case further stated, "Joint custody is rarely in the best interests of the child and should be decreed only under extraordinary circumstances." Although there are no specific "con" rulings on joint custody (as yet) in the District of Columbia, Maryland, or Virginia, you can be sure that the courts will agree pretty much with the Illinois and Vermont courts.

But if you want to go ahead with joint custody as being the best route for you, your spouse, and children, the following are eight criteria the court most likely will consider:

(1) The fitness of each parent as custodian;

(2) The children's psychological and emotional need for each parent as custodian;

(3) The ability of the parents to communicate with each other regarding the children's needs;

(4) Whether the parents have actively cared for the children before the separation;

(5) Whether each parent can be supportive of the other's relationship with the children;

(6) The children's wishes, ages, and maturity;

(7) Whether the parent's agree to joint custody; and,

(8) The geographic proximity of the parents' residences.

In some rare, but nevertheless true circumstances, courts have awarded joint custody to the parents even though they did not seek it, want it, or request it.

*How Joint
Custody
Works*

Joint custody can work in several ways. The parents can maintain homes within walking distance from each other, and they can simply both be available to the children. Or, the parents can actually split the custody of the children on a school year basis, such as one parent having the children during the school term and the other having custody the remaining 185 days. Another example is to maintain a family home in which the wife resides for six months followed by the husband taking over residence the remaining six months. Finally, the parents can rotate custody every year, generally with the children remaining in the same house.

Innocent Versus Guilty Parent

Although women are heavily penalized for committing adultery (by being denied alimony in most cases), the story changes when it comes to child custody. Even if the divorce is granted to the father—the mother being the guilty party in the divorce action—most courts still favor giving the mother custody of the children, although the father's right to custody is gaining more acceptance.

Children's Choosing Parents

If child custody becomes a contested matter, the court will, on occasion, listen to the wishes of a child, particularly a child of ten years or more. This does not necessarily mean that the child will be called into court as a witness. Most judges will try to talk to the child in chambers without the parents and their attorneys present in order to spare him or her the emotional trauma of testifying in the parent's divorce case. The child's wishes are given careful consideration but generally will not be the basis for determining which parent gets custody. However, if a court refuses to hear the testimony of a child in an appropriate case, or makes no effort to ascertain the child's wishes, that may constitute reversible error. For purposes of possible appeal of a custody order, the child's wishes should be made part of the record.

Visitation

Visitation may be at any time. One day a week and two weekends a month are customary, and a more frequently chosen visitation time is every other weekend, alternate holidays and a month during the summer vacation. The right of visitation is for the noncustodial parent, and your lawyer should draw up the rights and times of visitation and include it in your property settlement agreement. It could be, for example, every Sunday, every weekend, or every summer or school vacation. It's something both parents have to decide and agree upon. You can even set the exact times, such as from 9 A.M. to 8 P.M.

51

What If You Want to Move	If there are children involved in your divorce case, then no matter how much you hate Scaggsville, you can't simply pack up and move to Teaneck. You may have to have the court's permission to do so, because your move will be denying your spouse his or her visitation rights. It is becoming more and more common now for noncustodial spouses to insist in their separation agreements that the custodial spouse remain within a certain radius—such as 200 miles—of their former family home or that one spouse cannot take the children away for any longer than a specified period of time. In one case, a Swedish woman married to an American man was restricted from taking her child out of the country for more than six weeks. She can't simply bag it and move back to Sweden. If she does, she will be in contempt of court and could lose custody of her child.
Child Support	The laws emphatically state that it is the noncustodial parent's responsibility to contribute to the support of the minor children if financially capable. This obligation can terminate when any of the following events occur: the child dies; the child reaches legal adulthood; the child becomes self-supporting; the child marries; or becomes otherwise emancipated. Laws specifically state that child support is an equal obligation of both parents. If the father can't afford to pay for everything, the mother simply has to pitch in to help, which may mean learning a new skill or reviving an old one and going off to work.
Determining Child Support	Child support is determined in much the same way that alimony is: on the basis of the child's reasonable needs. Figure out how much you pay for clothing, food, doctors and dentists, incidentals such as Girl Scout uniforms and Little League equipment, and special costs such as school field-day trips, camps, and private lessons. Again, as with alimony, try to be reasonable. No matter how grossly you feel your spouse treated you, there's no point in trying to financially cripple him or her. It is not uncommon for people to try to use their children as a financial leverage in a divorce case, and this is of no benefit to anyone, particularly the children.

Child
Support
Payments

Child support payments are made to the court or parent who has custody of the child, and a precise time for payment (such as every Friday) should be incorporated into your property settlement agreement and divorce decree. Both parents should keep accurate records of when and how much child support is paid. If you're the payer, it's a good idea to pay by check so that if your spouse gets nasty at some later date and claims you didn't pay up, you'll have the canceled checks as proof. If you're on the receiving end of the line, keep a log of when and how much you were paid. How child support is used is another story. Often it'll come with the same check that takes care of alimony, and the parent with custody has the right to determine how it is spent.

The District of Columbia and Virginia specifically have ruled that child support is the duty of the parents, and in two cases where grandparents contributed substantially to their grandchildren's welfare, the father's obligation wasn't reduced at all. It was not a matter of how much was paid but who paid it. Cases in Virginia and Maryland have held that the father's voluntary contributions to his kids didn't reduce his duty to pay the agreed-upon child support. You can't take your children out, buy them half the contents of a toy store or clothing department, and expect not to pay child support that week or month.

In Virginia, a father does not have to support a crippled or disabled child if the child qualifies for and receives aid for the permanently or totally disabled. But in Maryland, if the child is disabled the father may be required to support the child through adulthood.

Agreements
to Modify or
Abate
Support

Should your spouse agree that your payments of support (spousal, child, or both) be reduced or temporarily or permanently abated, *keep paying* until and unless that agreement is reduced to writing as an addendum to your agreement or as a court order. A Virginia case has upheld the right of one party to seek redress through the courts and to collect back payments due for support where an earlier oral agreement allegedly reduced support payments, but no written change was ever entered as part of the court record. The same holds true where a paying father gave checks for support to his spouse payable to the children and not to the wife. The courts are strict to adhere to the requirement that support obligations are payable to the spouse directly. Failure to do so may result in a finding by the court that, although your spouse received and cashed those monthly checks totalling $3,000, they were merely "gifts" because you made them payable to your minor children and not directly to your spouse. On top of your "gifts" (which you thought were your support payments) the court may find you in contempt of court as well as ordering you to pay another $3,000 for back support payable to your spouse.

Should your children begin to reside with you, by agreement between you and your spouse, see your lawyer's office to insure that the custody agreement, including the change in support obligations or termination of those obligations is properly recorded in the appropriate court file. While you may be feeling secure and happy that the children are now with you, the court may later tell you that your failure to change the existing support order, *post haste*, has resulted in your accruing an enormous back support obligation. Your spouse may be entitled to a sudden windfall profit while you are busy with the children.

When Support Isn't Paid

Since child support payments are incorporated in either the property settlement agreement, an interim order, or the divorce decree, the payments remain within the control of the court until the child becomes an adult, and occasionally afterward as well. No matter what the agreement states about child support, the court can always change it.

It is not uncommon for the noncustodial parent to skip child-support payments. The national average of chronic child support delinquency is between 65 to 80 per cent. It is so common that area jurisdictions have enacted laws to make child support collection easier.

In the District of Columbia, child-support orders issued after January 1, 1984 may be enforced by the D.C. Superior Court. This, however, does not apply to welfare recipients whose cases are handled by the city government.

In order to benefit from the new laws, the custodial spouses should ask that the court monitor the payments, which are then made directly to the court. The system is computerized so that if a payment is not made, the errant parent will receive a court notice demanding payment plus a $5 late fee. If payment is not made within 10 days, the court automatically will move to garnishee the spouse's wages, including a $50 fine to cover court costs.

Under the new law, the court can garnishee up to 50 per cent of the person's wages. However, the D.C. Superior Court can initiate garnishment proceedings in the District only.

Similar systems also exist in Baltimore, Fairfax County and Prince George's County.

If your county does not help you in enforcing child support payments and you know where your spouse resides, you can go to your lawyer and ask that a Petition for a Rule to Show Cause be filed. Your spouse will have to appear before the court and explain why he or she should not be held in contempt of court. If the person isn't acceptable to the judge, then the spouse could be sent to prison. Although a prison sentence might satisfy your vengeful instincts, it usually won't pay the rent or clothe and feed the children. But in Virginia, you could get $100 to $125 a month from your spouse's earnings on the state convict road force. Still, you need other ways to get what is owed you.

Garnish-
ment

A spouse may file a lawsuit against the unpaying spouse and ask that the amount owed be reduced to a judgment against the spouse. If the spouse who brings the action wins, then the nonpaying spouse's salary may be garnished which means that the nonpaying spouse's employer will withhold specified amounts out of each paycheck. The spouse then receives a check from the employer. Federal government employees, however, are exempt from having their salaries garnisheed thanks—or no thanks—to the Federal Employees Compensation Act.

Uniform
Reciprocal
Enforcement
of Support
Act

If your spouse has left the state, you can turn to the powers of the Uniform Reciprocal Enforcement of Support Act, whether or not you know where he is living. Every state has adopted the act as a law. Here's how it works: if your spouse lives in a different state from the one you live in, you have to call the clerk's office at your local Court of Domestic Relations to learn who will file a "Reciprocal Non-Support Petition." In the District of Columbia, the special litigation division of the Corporation Counsel's office handles the enforcement of the act. In Maryland, the county attorney's office handles it if the mother is residing in the state and the father is not. But the state's attorney's office handles it if the father is a Maryland resident and the mother is not. In Virginia, the clerk at the Juvenile and

Domestic Relations Court will file the petition against the father in whatever Virginia jurisdiction he resides in.

Once caught, the father will have to appear before the court, explain his reasons for nonsupport, and reach an agreement with the court as to back and future alimony and child support payments. The Uniform Reciprocal Enforcement of Support Act provides for a nonpaying spouse residing in a different state to be served with your petition for nonsupport, and to make his/her court appearance in the state of his/her current residence.

Child Support Collection Program

Effective April 4, 1982 there is a requirement that there must be a minimum of $750 in delinquent child support payments before IRS assistance can be brought into play. In addition a state child support enforcement agency must have made reasonable efforts at collection before a referral to the federal agency can be made. All requests for IRS collection also require the debtor's social security number as well as a verification of the last known address and place of employment of the debtor.

In order for the service to be effective, of course, the debtor has to have employment in which he or she uses the correct social security number. Many do. In 1982, The Internal Revenue Service intercepted over 323,000 tax-refund checks amounting to $170,200,000 under the Child Support Collection Program.

Taxes and Child Support

Child support is neither tax deductible nor taxable. Often, the only tax relief for child support payments is for the parent who can file for a dependency exemption. Obviously, both parents can't claim their children as dependents, so it has to be agreed on by you, your spouse, and the Internal Revenue Service as to who gets to claim the kids. Generally, if both parents contribute like amounts to their children's support, the parent who has custody of the children gets to claim them as dependents. However, if the noncustodial parent contributes over half of the child's actual support requirements, he or she can claim the deduction. The IRS also requires that if the noncustodial parent is claiming the deduction, he or she must attach a copy of the agreement to the income tax form.

The Lester Plan

A roundabout way of getting to deduct child support payments from your income taxes is to call it alimony. This is known as the Lester Plan. Both parties will have to agree to it, and the wife must remember that she will have to pay taxes on the money. There have been many wives who have agreed to higher alimony payment and lower child support payments because they found that overall their husbands would give them a much greater amount, since Uncle Sam is in effect paying part of it. The following are examples of how the Lester Plan works.

The examples assume that the husband has a gross income of $24,000 a year, the wife having no income other than alimony and child support. The calculation is based on the 1983 income tax rate for "single tax payer" for the husband, and "unmarried heads of household" rates for the wife. You should be aware that this does not take into account the various deductions, including sales, gas, state, and local taxes, or the personal exemption. It merely is a rough outline and indicates that if the husband were to pay $500 per month to his wife, with $200 per month representing alimony and $300 reprsenting child support, then his disposable income would be almost equal to a situation in which he would be paying $700 a month as alimony under the Lester Plan. You will also note that if the husband pays $1,000 per month to his wife under the Lester provision, their disposable net incomes are equal (see example No. 4).

Examples

HUSBAND

$24,000—Husband's Annual Income
1. Husband pays to Wife $500 per month, $200 as alimony and $300 as child support.
   $24,000 Annual Income
   <u> 2,400</u> (12 mos. × $200)—Alimony Deduction
   $21,600 Taxable Income
   Tax on $21,600 = $2,865 + 28% (3400) = 2865 + 952 = $3,817
   After payment of federal taxes:
   $24,000 Annual Income
   <u> 6,000</u> (12 mos. × $500)—Alimony and Child Support
   $18,000
   <u> 3,817</u> Taxes
   $14,183 Disposable Income of Husband

2. Husband pays to Wife $700 per month as support and maintenance for herself and the child, under Lester provision.

$24,000 Annual Income

<u>8,400</u> (12 mos. × $700)—Alimony and Child Support Deduction

$15,600 Taxable Income

Tax on $15,600 = $2,097 + 24% (600) = 2097 + 144 = $2,241

After payment of federal taxes:

$24,000 Annual Income

<u>8,400</u> Alimony and Child Support

$15,600

<u>2,241</u> Taxes

$13,359 Disposable Income of Husband

3. Husband pays to Wife $800 per month as support and maintenance for herself and the child, under Lester provision.

$24,000 Annual Income

<u>9,600</u> (12 mos. × $800)—Alimony and Child Support

$14,400 Taxable Income

Tax on $14,400 = $1,656 + 21% (1500) = 1656 + 315 = $1,971

After payment of federal taxes:

$24,000 Annual Income

<u>9,600</u> Alimony and Child Support

$14,400

<u>1,971</u> Taxes

$12,429 Disposable Income of Husband

4. Husband pays to Wife $1,000 per month as support and maintenance for herself and the child, under Lester provision.

$24,000 Annual Income

<u>12,000</u> (12 mos. × $1000)—Alimony and Child Support Deduction

$12,000 Taxable Income

Tax on $12,000 = $1,257 + 19% (1200) = 1257 + 228 = $1,485

After payment of federal taxes:

$24,000 Annual Income

<u>12,000</u> Alimony and Child Support

$12,000

<u>1,485</u> Taxes

$10,515 Disposable Income of Husband

Examples

WIFE

1. Wife receives from Husband $500 per month, $200 as alimony and $300 as child support.
   $6,000 Alimony and Child Support
   <u>3,600</u> Child Support
   $2,400 Taxable Income
   Tax on $2,400 = 11% × 100 = $11
   After payment of federal taxes:
   $6,000 Alimony and Child Support
   <u>11</u> Taxes
   $5,989 Disposable Income of Wife
2. Wife receives from Husband $700 per month as support and maintenance for herself and the child under Lester provision.
   $8,400—Alimony and Child Support—Taxable Income
   Tax on $8,400 = $504 + 15% (1900) = 504 + 285 = $789
   After payment of federal taxes:
   $8,400 Alimony and Child Support
   <u>789</u> Taxes
   $7,611 Disposable Income of Wife
3. Wife receives from Husband $800 per month as support and maintenance for herself and the child under Lester provision.
   $9,600—Alimony and Child Support—Taxable Income
   Tax on $9,600 = $834 + 18% (900) = 834 + 162 = $996
   After payment of federal taxes:
   $9,600 Alimony and Child Support
   <u>996</u> Taxes
   $8,604 Disposable Income of Wife
4. Wife receives from Husband $1,000 per month as support and maintenance for herself and the child under Lester provision.
   $12,000—Alimony and Child Support—Taxable Income
   Tax on $12,000 = $1,392 + 19% (200) = 1,392 + 38 = $1,430
   After payment of federal taxes:
   $12,000 Alimony and Child Support
   <u>1,430</u> Taxes
   $10,570 Disposable Income of Wife

Parental *Child* *Snatching*	By now, most people have either read or heard the grim, painful stories or have seen at least one movie of parents snatching their children away from the other parent. In response to this relatively new occurrence of the noncustodial parent illegally taking the children away from the custodial parent, the federal government has made a small step in the direction of relief. This relief takes the form of the Parental Kidnapping Prevention Act of 1980, better known as PKPA. But here's a bit of "off the record" background.

The federal government really has no desire to get involved in marital or divorce squabbles. Basically, federal legislators feel that domestic matters are best left to the individual states to handle according to their laws. But as parental child snatching became more prevalent, more pressure was placed on the federal government to do something about this new quote-unquote crime. The result is PKPA.

Parent *Locator* *Service*

Here's how PKPA works—or doesn't work—depending on your interpretation of it. PKPA provides that each state in the Union may enter into an agreement with the federal government's Office of Child Support Enforcement (OCSE) at the discretion of the state. The OCSE, in turn, can provide the state with access to the Federal Parental Locator Service (PLS). The PLS contains nationwide social security information which once was used only to locate nonsupporting spouses for child support or to establish paternity. Now, however, the PKPA grants access to the Parental Locator Services for cases involving child custody and parental kidnapping.

Now for the rub: The decision to use the Parent Locator Service is up to the state. That may not seem too difficult except for the fact that the federal government has set up some rather strict rules that the states must follow in order to use the service. First of all, the state must collect or pay the fees required for processing requests made to the Parent Locator Service. Keep in mind here that most states are not anxious to give up state funds, particularly in what they might consider to be a family matter.

The state also must agree with the federal government that the state will impose, collect, and account for fees to offset the federal processing costs, as well as to send OCSE's portion of the fee to it when billed. Finally, the state must agree to restrict access to the data received, to store it securely, and to take all other necessary precautions to insure its confidentiality.

The result is pretty much the same as the starting point: the federal government has passed a law that satisfies its obligation of showing concern, but it still leaves what recourse there is up to the states. The bottom line is that custodial parents whose children have been kidnapped by the noncustodial spouse should attempt to find their children through private means as well as through the courts.

Alimony/Spousal Support

Alimony, which stems from the Latin meaning "to nourish," has had such a bad press that it is now referred to as "support and maintenance" or "spousal support." The popular myth concerning alimony is that the wife ends up living regally in suburbia while the penniless husband is fated to a cheap hotel existence. That is far from the truth. First, alimony is awarded in only 15 to 17 per cent of all divorce cases. Second, every study on the subject has consistently shown that it is the wife or homemaker whose standard of living drops drastically—by about two-thirds. Third, the trend today is toward temporary or "rehabilitative" alimony—alimony that only lasts a specified period of time. Finally, alimony no longer "belongs" to women. In the District of Columbia, Maryland and Virginia, it is awarded to the dependent spouse in a marriage regardless of gender.

If you were to let the court decide on the amount of alimony, the following would be taken into consideration:

1. How long you were married.
2. How many dependent children you have.
3. Your present income and earning ability.
4. Your age and general health.
5. Your standard of living.

6. Your ground for divorce.
7. Your assets and liabilities.
8. Your education and training, or your ability to secure such education and training.
9. You and your spouse's tax consequences.
10. Your contribution to the well being of your family, financial and nonfinancial.
11. Your prior working experience and that of your spouse.
12. Other facts which your lawyer and the court may deem important.

If you haven't been married very long and have no children, and both you and your spouse were employed during your marriage, then alimony probably would not be awarded at all.

If the marriage lasted for several years, there are children, and the wife is financially dependent on the husband, the only question concerning alimony may be how much. Children, particularly young children, often make the difference as to whether alimony is paid and how much. The "I-have-to-stay-home-with-the-children" line rarely failed in the past to evoke a sympathetic judicial ear. Now, however, the court may not be as inclined to award spousal support on that basis.

Present income, as well as the ability to earn, is also an important consideration. If, for example, the husband or wife is in training to be a computer programmer, it's reasonable to assume that present income is less than what it will be after complete training. Alimony payments may well be based on future income.

Age also makes a difference in the amount of payments. Since younger people have more of a chance to earn a better living than, for example, someone starting a career at age 50, alimony will be awarded accordingly. The same thing is true of health. If you are in good health, the court will consider you more able to earn your own living. In Virginia, it's even a misdemeanor for a woman not to support her ex-spouse if he's aged, infirm, or disabled. She could be fined up to $500 or imprisoned for one year, or both, if convicted.

The ground for divorce also is important. In Virginia a finding of fault sufficient to allow a divorce to be granted on any ground that casts blame for the breakup of the marriage is adequate to result in alimony being denied.

Types of Alimony (MD)

In Maryland, there is a distinction made regarding alimony. There are two types of alimony. The first is technical alimony which is subject to being increased or decreased as circumstances warrant. The second type of alimony is fixed alimony which a court cannot modify regardless of any change in circumstances. Assume that your spouse gets sick or loses his or her job and has no source of income. With a provision for fixed alimony, your spouse cannot go to court and request that the alimony be reduced, suspended, or in any way modified. What constitutes fixed alimony depends on the language used in the separation agreement spelling out the terms and duration of the alimony. It is for such a technical point that one must have counsel to properly use the "magic words" to get what you truly want.

How Much to Ask For

Unless you are very wealthy, you probably cannot maintain the same standard of living. It will have to go down some. No one would expect you to move from a five-bedroom house to an efficiency apartment, but a three-bedroom house wouldn't be considered unreasonable.

The most important things in determining the amount of your alimony are your needs and your ability to be reasonable. It will not help anyone to try to get even financially.

To determine the amount of your alimony, figure out how much you spend on each monthly living expense. The following list is a fairly standard one and operates as a guideline for those expenses which may be taken into consideration by a court in determining a spousal support award.

FINANCIAL STATEMENT OF _____

Children: _____ Ages _____ Custody _____

	EXPENSES $/week			EXPENSES $/week
I. Household:		II.	Food:	
Rent or mortgage	_____		Staples	_____
Property taxes	_____		Dining out	_____
Gas/Electric/ phone	_____	III.	Transportation:	
Water/sewage/ trash	_____		Auto payments	_____
Heating	_____		Auto insurance	_____

	EXPENSES $/week			EXPENSES $/week
Gas & Oil	_____		Books	_____
Maintenance & repairs	_____		Lunches	_____
Tires, tags etc	_____		Activities	
IV. Clothing:			Fees	_____
Plaintiff	_____		Allowances	_____
Children	_____		Recreation	_____
Laundry/dry cleaning	_____		Hairstyling	_____
Special/uniforms	_____	VIII.	Gifts	
V. Medical Expenses			Birthday	_____
Doctor/Dentist	_____		Christmas	_____
Prescriptions	_____		Church	_____
Drug Store items	_____		Other	_____
Other medical	_____	IX.	Sundries	
VI. Insurance			Newspapers/ magazines	_____
Medical/Hospital	_____		Grooming (hair/cosmetics)	_____
Life	_____		Maid	_____
Homeowner's	_____	X.	Miscellaneous	
VII. Children's School			Yard work	_____
Tuition	_____		babysitter	_____
Room & Board	_____		nursery school	_____
Transportation	_____		Other	_____
Uniforms	_____			_____
				_____
				_____
				_____
				_____
				_____
		TOTAL EXPENSES ABOVE		_____

INCOME

Wages	_____
Income from Property	_____
Other income (other than spouse)	_____
TOTAL INCOME above	_____
LESS TOTAL EXPENSES ABOVE	_____
NET INCOME	_____

Review your checkbook over the last two years and add up your expenditures under the categories listed above. As a single person, you may need more or less, depending on the categories. Your food bills may go down but your insurance and entertainment expenses are likely to go up. When you figure out a yearly total, add an additional 10 per cent for inflation and another 5 to 10 per cent for savings—both of which are reasonable.

Escalating Alimony

Historically, the cost of living goes up, not down. So what do you do if you are living on a fixed income of alimony payments, which is your only means of support? You could ask for an escalation agreement. Your spouse's income, like everything else, is likely to go up. You could ask for 5 to 10 per cent of your spouse's net or gross raise, if and when one is given. The argument for this is that your cost of living is going up and you need more money to meet those costs, particularly if you have children. You may also agree upon an escalator clause governed by the current Consumer Price Index published by the U.S. Department of Labor.

Percentage Alimony

You could also ask for alimony that is based on a percentage of your spouse's income. You could ask for 30 to 40 per cent of his income, depending on your financial needs and his earnings. The benefit of the percentage plan is that you will get an automatic increase whenever your ex-spouse gets a raise. The disadvantage is that if he gets demoted or takes a lower-paying job, your alimony will go down too.

Lump Sum Alimony

You could settle for a lump sum amount either as alimony or given in lieu of it. This type of payment is especially good for people who have their own incomes but who might want a compensation for the property division (such as $500 for the silverware), or for women who are planning to remarry soon. The lump sum payment, which actually can be spread out over a period of years, is not tax deductible or taxable, unless it is extended over ten years or longer.

Rehabilitative Alimony

If left to most courts, you probably would be awarded what is known as "rehabilitative alimony." This is a temporary form of alimony payable for a period of six months, one year, or more. It is the court's answer to helping you get back on your feet again. It is paid to you only for a specific period of time so that you may look for work if you are able to, or take the time to learn new job skills, or return to school to further your ability to support yourself. This is now the most common form of spousal support. It's distinguishing characteristic is the short period of time for which it is awarded—usually no more than two years.

Taxes and Alimony The Giver

Even alimony has a silver lining and it comes in the form of tax breaks. Any alimony that you pay is tax deductible (child support payments are not deductible but you could claim the children as dependents). You can deduct the full amount of alimony that you have paid for the year from your gross income, which will give you a lower net income on which to pay taxes.

The Receiver

To keep things even, the Internal Revenue Service expects the recipient of alimony to pay taxes on it. It is viewed as income, just as if it were wages received from a job. The only difference—and it could be important—is that no taxes are withheld from it.

If you do receive substantial alimony and it is your only source of income, you must file quarterly estimated returns so that you can spread out your tax payments over the year. For additional information see Taxes and Child Support on page 56.

Giving Up Alimony

You should be advised that once you give up alimony, you relinquish all claims to it forever. You might want to ask for a nominal amount of alimony, such as one dollar or two dollars a month. If you ever need money in the event of an emergency, such as a serious illness, you could ask the court to raise your alimony to cover your expenses. In some jurisdictions the court can reserve the right to have alimony awarded at a later date.

Temporary Alimony

All courts have the power to grant temporary alimony, known as *Pendente Lite* alimony, before your case is actually heard. Your lawyers by agreement or the court can set the amount, which is based on the same considerations as is permanent alimony. The purpose of temporary alimony is to cover the spouse's expenses—regardless of whether the spouse is the defendant or plaintiff—until the case comes to court. The problem with temporary alimony is that the amount that is set is rarely lowered after the case comes to trial. It often turns into "permanent" alimony, so you should consider this when setting the temporary amount.

Change of
Fortunes

Until recently, either party was able to petition the court to ask that alimony payments be increased, decreased, or stopped altogether. Now this is true only in the District of Columbia. In Maryland, if the alimony is considered to be "fixed" alimony, usually only the husband's death can make a difference in the payments (they obviously would cease). But, if it's considered "technical" alimony, the court is still controlling the helm. (See page 21. for definitions of fixed and technical alimony.)

In Virginia, if alimony is agreed to in the property settlement agreement and the agreement is incorporated into the final decree, then the court doesn't have the power to change a dime of it. But if a Virginia court set the amount of alimony, it maintains complete control as to whether it can be raised, lowered, or halted.

When
Alimony
Ends

The death of either party or remarriage of the wife terminates alimony, unless the property settlement agreement states otherwise.

Your Day In Court

Although divorce cases are a matter of public record and, as such, are open to anyone who is interested, divorce hearings are still rather private.

In the District of Columbia, the majority of the uncontested cases are heard in the privacy of the Hearing Commissioner's office. Generally, the only people present are you, your lawyer (if you have one), your witness, and the defense attorney. The atmosphere, unlike that in a courtroom, is relaxed and even congenial.

In the Washington metropolitan area, Maryland uncontested divorce cases are heard by Masters of Domestic Relations in small, open-to-the-public courtrooms. But don't worry about a lack of privacy. Most of the people in the courtroom are there for the same reason—to get their own divorce.

Virginia uncontested divorce cases in the metropolitan area are heard by Commissioners in Chancery, who hold the hearings in their own law offices. You, your lawyer, your witness, the Commissioner, and a court reporter are the only persons present.

In rural areas of Maryland and Virginia, divorces may be heard at the county or local courthouse by judges.

Your
"Judge"
Call him "Your Honor," but the person who is most likely to hear your uncontested divorce case is not a judge, particularly in the Washington metropolitan area, Baltimore, and Richmond. He is a judicial intermediary, a kind of go-between for the people and the judge. He does not have the power to grant a divorce, but he does have the power

69

to make recommendations that a case either be accepted or denied. But don't worry. Probably 95 per cent of the cases go through to a final decree.

Your Court

In the District of Columbia, your court is the Superior Court of the District of Columbia, located at 451 Indiana Avenue, N.W. In Maryland, you will go to the County Courthouse, and in Virginia, your "court" will be at the Commissioner in Chancery's private law office. Be sure that you show up exactly on time. If you're late, you may have to wait a few months to get another court date. Regardless of how good your excuse is, most courts will not wait for you.

Your Witness

All contested and uncontested divorce cases require that you have one or more witnesses, who are necessary to corroborate or verify the circumstances of your divorce case. In uncontested cases, the witness verifies your residency, your date of separation, the fact that you and your spouse are no longer living and cohabitating together, that the separation has been voluntary and continuous, and that there is no hope for a reconciliation.

Choosing a Witness

Your witness can be almost anyone: a friend, a parent, a neighbor, a relative, even your grown children. Your witness should be someone who knows you and your situation well and, also, someone whom you can trust.

At the Hearing

Make sure that your file contains all the forms listed on pages 93–98. In the District of Columbia and Maryland, you also must bring a certified copy of your marriage certificate with you.

Questions at the Hearing The Plaintiff

The following questions, with slight variations in wording, will usually be asked the plaintiff at the hearing. However, if you are *pro se*, it's a good idea to have a statement prepared giving all the necessary information in case the judge won't ask the questions himself. Many *pro se*-ers will ask themselves the questions and then provide their own answers.

Sample answers follow in parentheses.

1. Please state your name and address. (Selma Barnes Does, 2829—68th Street, N.W., Washington, D.C.)

2. How long have you been a resident of the District of Columbia, Maryland, or Virginia? (Three years.)
3. Has your residency been continuous? (Yes.)
4. Did there come a time when you became married? (Yes.)
5. To whom? (Gunnar Does.)
6. When and where was that? (October 6, 1970, in Fairfield, Connecticut.)
7. Can you identify this document? The marriage certificate is handed to you. (Yes, it is my marriage certificate, which I enter to the court as evidence.)
8. Were there any children born of this marriage? (Yes.) (If NO, the next two questions are omitted.)
9. What are their names and ages? (Peter Steven Does, age 3.)
10. Who has custody of the child? (I do.)
11. Did there come a time when you and your husband agreed to separate? (Yes.)
12. When was that? (On May 1, 1983.)
13. Where were you living at the time of separation? (At 2829—68th Street, N.W., Washington, D.C.)
14. Who left? (My husband Gunnar Does.)
15. Why did you separate? (We could not get along and agreed to go our separate ways.)
16. Has this separation been voluntary, continuous, and uninterrupted for more than a year? (Yes.)
17. Are you (or is your husband) a fit and proper person to have custody of your minor child? (Yes.)
18. Are there any property rights to be settled by the Court? (No.)
19. Is there any reasonable hope or expectation for a reconciliation? (No.)
20. In Virginia, you are likely to be asked, "Are you over the age of 18?" (Yes.)
21. Have provisions been made for the support of your minor child? (Yes, my husband has agreed to pay me $75 a week.)

The Witness Your witness is then asked the following questions by a commissioner, or you can ask the questions yourself. Sample answers follow in parentheses.

1. Please state your name and address. (Gina Adolphson, 3107 Julia Drive, Arlington, Virginia.)
2. How long have you known the plaintiff? (Five years.)

3. Where does the plaintiff live? (2829—68th Street, N.W., Washington, D.C.)

4. How long has the plaintiff been a resident of the District of Columbia (or Maryland or Virginia)? (Three years.)

5. Did there come a time when you learned that the parties separated? (Yes.)

6. When and how did you learn about it? (Selma told me that she and her husband agreed to separate. It was in May, 1983. A few weeks later I saw Gunnar Does and he told me that he and Selma agreed to separate.)

7. Do you have occasion to visit the plaintiff? (Yes.)

8. How often? (About every two weeks.)

9. Have you seen the defendant or any evidence of his living there? (No.)

10. If he was living there would you know it? (Yes!)

11. Do you feel that she is a fit and proper person to have custody of Peter Steven Does? (Yes.)

12. In Virginia, the witness is likely to be asked, "Are the parties over the age of 18?" (Yes.)

13. Do you feel that there is any hope for reconciliation? (No.)

End of Hearing

It is extremely important that neither the plaintiff nor the witness give any more information than is asked for. There have been many cases where the divorce did not go through because people started to talk too much. Picture this: "Have you seen the defendant or any evidence of his living there?" (Well, a lot of his clothes are still there. And his stereo. And I have seen him over there a couple of times. Just a couple of months ago, he was over having breakfast with Selma.) An answer like that could cause the Hearing Commissioner to stop or rescind the divorce action. This does not mean that you should lie, which is perjury. Just be sure to answer the questions simply and directly.

Also, in Virginia cases, there is a great deal of stress on residency, such as, "How long have you lived in Virginia?," "Have you ever left the state and lived elsewhere?" and similar questions regarding the defendant's residency in the state (particularly if you are filing in the county in which the defendant resides).

The Judgment

There comes the day when you feel that finally it's over. You go to court, tell your story, and walk out of the courtroom thinking that you're a free person. Guess again. In the District of Columbia, your uncontested divorce probably will be heard by the Hearing Commissioner. The Hearing Commissioner will make certain findings of facts and conclusions of law at the end of your hearing, and you will provide the Hearing Commissioner with a document entitled Findings of Fact, Conclusions of Law, and Judgment of Absolute Divorce. This is known as your Judgment of Divorce (see forms). The Hearing Commissioner will sign the judgment, which will, at that time, be sent to the judge in chambers. It may then take two or three days before the actual judgment has been signed by a judge of the Superior Court for the District of Columbia. Once the judgment has been signed, you should receive a post card from the Clerk's Office indicating that a Judgment of Absolute Divorce was entered on the docket on whatever date it was. That date is critical to you. For all intents and purposes, it is the day that you are legally divorced. However, the judgment does not become final until the time for taking an appeal has expired. (Of course, there should be no appeal from an uncontested divorce, since an uncontested divorce implies that there are no issues in dispute between the parties.)

73

In the District of Columbia, the waiting period is 60 days from the date your judgment was docketed or put down in the court records. If you plan to remarry immediately, you must wait until those 60 days are up. If you or or your spouse files a Notice of Appeal in the meantime, then that would stay the finality of the divorce. If any portion of the Judgment of Absolute Divorce is appealed to the District of Columbia Court of Appeals, you are not divorced until the appeal has been disposed of. The situation is somewhat the same in Maryland and Virginia.

In Maryland, a Master for Domestic Relations or Examiner in Chancery will hear your divorce case. He will make recommendations to the court, which must be provided in a Decree for Absolute Divorce that is signed by him and then signed by a judge of the Circuit Court. Again, as in the District of Columbia, the decree is docketed and there is, at that time, 30 days in which to note an appeal. You cannot remarry until the 30 days have expired, unless it is an uncontested case.

In Virginia, your divorce is final as soon as the judge signs the decree. You can remarry the next minute, unless an appeal is filed. But there is a bit of a rub. There are 30 days in which to take an appeal, and if the appeal is successful, your second marriage may be voided.

Limitations in the Meantime

Until your divorce is final, your legal status is that of one who is married. You should also be aware that just because you've signed that voluntary separation agreement, it does not necessarily mean that your spouse can't obtain a divorce on other grounds. You will note from the sample separation agreements (see pages 28–44) that there is a provision that the parties reserve the right to file for a divorce for any cause or ground that either of them may have against the other party. Even though you may have agreed to a voluntary separation, that does not preclude your spouse from filing for a divorce on the grounds of adultery. The same could be true if a divorce was actually heard and a judgment was entered. If your spouse appeals and the Court of Appeals holds that the judgment be set aside and orders a new trial, your spouse could file under a different ground, such as adultery, for divorce. This is unlikely, but it has happened and you should be aware of the possibility.

How and When Your Divorce can be Overturned

Your divorce can be overturned in a variety of ways, although all are quite remote. A divorce action is an equity action, in which the judge acts as both judge and jury. In order to overturn the decision of the judge, the Court of Appeals must find that he acted in a manner that is "arbitrary and capricious." Days could be spent defining what could be considered arbitrary and capricious, but basically, it is the types of Findings of Facts that negate common sense and are extremely unreasonable. It is very difficult, however, to overturn a lower court decision in a divorce case.

Glossary Of Legal Terms

AB INITIO—Latin for "from the beginning."

AFFIDAVIT—a written statement under oath.

ALIAS SUMMONS—another summons when the original is not served on the defendant.

A MENSA ET THORO—from the Latin meaning "from bed and board." It is a legal separation honored by the courts. It is also known as a limited divorce or a legal separation.

ANNULMENT—a marriage can be dissolved in a legal proceeding in which the marriage is declared void, as though it never took place. In the eyes of the law, the parties were never married. Each state has its own grounds for annulment.

ANSWER—the papers filed with the court by the defendant responding to the plaintiff's Bill of Complaint. The answer gives the defendant the legal right to admit or deny his or her innocence. Maryland and Virginia do not require an answer in a divorce case. The District of Columbia does.

A VINCULO MATRIMONII—Latin for "from the bonds of matrimony." It is a full-fledged, legal divorce.

COLLUSION—an agreement between two or more persons that one of the parties bring false charges against the other. In a divorce case, the husband and wife may agree to use adultery as a ground in order to obtain a divorce more quickly, knowing full well that adultery was not committed. Collusion is illegal.

COMMISSIONER IN CHANCERY—a court-appointed lawyer who serves as a legal intermediary in Virginia divorce cases. He hears the case and makes the recommendation to the court as to whether or not the divorce should be granted.

COMPLAINANT—the one who files the suit, same as plaintiff.

COMPLAINT—called the Bill of Complaint. It is the papers the plaintiff files with the court that brings forth the allegations or reasons why a divorce should be granted.

CONDONATION—the act of forgiving one's spouse who has committed an act of wrongdoing that would constitute a ground for divorce. Condonation generally is proven by living and cohabiting with the spouse after learning that the wrongdoing was committed. It often is used as a defense to a divorce.

CONNIVANCE—one party purposely and intentionally traps the other party into committing a wrongdoing so a divorce can be obtained. For example, a husband may try to trap his wife into committing adultery by setting her up with an old lover. If discovered, connivance bars a divorce. It also is used as a defense to a divorce.

CONSIDERATION—something of value in exchange for some act or thing of value. Essential element to a contract.

CONTEMPT or CONTEMPT OF COURT—the failure of one party to comply with an order of the court, which results in punishment such as a fine or jail sentence.

CONTESTED DIVORCE—the refusal by one party to the action to agree with the other, regardless of the reason, be it grounds, custody, or alimony.

CORESPONDENT—the person jointly charged with the defendant generally of having committed adultery. The corespondent also becomes a defendant in the case.

COURTESY—husband's one-third interest in wife's property in the District of Columbia and Virginia. See dower.

CUSTODY—the right to care for, educate, house, and keep the children or pets. The parent having custody rights is called the custodial parent. The other parent is called the noncustodial parent.

DECREE—the decision of an equity court.

DECREE PRO CONFESSO—in the event that the defendant does not answer the complaint within the specified period of time, the court may consider the defendant's silence as a Decree Pro Confesso —admission of guilt.

DEFAULT—the failure to comply with an obligation or to file an answer to the complaint.

DEFENDANT—the person who has been charged in a divorce suit. The defendant has the right to admit or deny the charges. In some states, the defendant is referred to as the "respondent."

DEPOSITION—an examination under oath reduced to writing used to preserve testimony or for obtaining information.

DOMICILE—the state that you consider to be your legal, permanent home as opposed to a temporary residence.

DOWER RIGHTS—wives in the District of Columbia and Virginia are granted a one-third interest in all their husband's real property. The wife loses interest in dower rights after the divorce, but they apply only upon the death of the husband.

EQUITY—the court of equity that has jurisdiction over divorce cases. A person filing suit in a court of equity must enter under the "clean hands" rule. That is, the person filing suit must not be guilty of any wrongdoings.

HEARING COMMISSIONER—a judicial intermediary who hears uncontested divorce cases in the District of Columbia. He has the power to recommend that a divorce be granted or denied.

IN FORMA PAUPERIS—Latin for "in the form of a pauper." Persons filing *In Forma Pauperis* must petition the court to ask that they be provided with free legal counsel. A detailed financial statement is a must.

INJUNCTION—a court order called a "mandatory injunction" forbidding a party to do something such as harassment, selling property, or even ordering a party to move out of the home, enforceable by contempt.

INTERROGATORIES—written questions from one party to another in a court action, which must be answered under oath.

JUDGMENT—the final decree of divorce stating that you are now free to go your own way, or it can deny your divorce action.

JOINT TENANCY—the ownership of property with another or several persons. For example, a husband and wife who have their home in both their names, own it by joint tenancy. When one spouse dies, the other spouse automatically becomes the full owner. When husband and wife hold title in this manner it is called a tenancy by the entireties.

LACHES—a form of statute of limitations in which a person who thinks he/she has the right to sue and would reasonably be expected to sue but doesn't. For example, if a wife has lived with an impotent husband for 35 years, she probably would be denied a divorce, as laches would be put into effect.

LIEN—a notice of a claim against a piece of property, warning prospective buyers that a claim must be paid from the proceeds of the sale. It can be used to collect back alimony and child support payments.

MASTER OF DOMESTIC RELATIONS—the judicial intermediary in Maryland who hears divorce cases and can recommend that they be granted or not.

NO FAULT—when neither party is guilty or at blame in a divorce action.

NOTARIZED—signed and sworn under oath before a Notary Public.

PENDENTE LITE—Latin for "pending the suit." It is the time prior to the suit or the time during which the suit is taking place. *Pendente Lite* alimony, child support, or custody can be awarded by the court.

PLAINTIFF—the person who initiates the suit against his or her spouse by filing a Bill of Complaint with the court. Also called "petitioner" in some states.

PRIMA FACIE—Latin for "at first sight." A case in which the evidence is strong enough for the defendant to answer to it.

PRO SE—Latin for "on behalf of oneself." Any person who represents his or herself in a court.

RETAINER—the initial deposit—usually nonrefundable—paid to your attorney at the beginning of your suit.

SEPARATION AGREEMENT—an agreement in which the parties put in writing their intent to separate and live apart. It also may contain provisions for the division of property. Also referred to as property settlement agreement.

SERVICE—the process by which the defendant is notified that a suit has been filed against him or her. Service may be by the personal delivery of the Bill by a United States marshal, process server, or sheriff, by the registered, return-receipt-requested mailing of the Bill, or by the written publication in a newspaper that a suit is taking place. The latter generally is used only in cases of actual desertion and when the whereabouts of the defendant are unknown.

SUMMONS—an order issued by the court after a complaint has been filed. The summons tells the defendant that a suit has been filed and specifies the period of time in which the defendant has to answer the complaint.

UNCONTESTED DIVORCE—a case in which both parties mutually agree to the divorce.

WAIVER—giving up a legal right, such as the right to alimony.

VENUE—the county or city within the state that has the power to hear the case.

Appendix

Grounds for Divorce and Residency Requirements for the Fifty States, the District of Columbia, Puerto Rico, and the Virgin Islands*

Alabama   Grounds: Impotency at time of marriage; adultery; physical violence; abandonment for one year; imprisonment in penitentiary for two years under sentence for seven years or more; crime against nature before or after marriage; habitual drunkenness or drug addiction contracted after marriage; five successive years in an insane asylum after marriage; irretrievable breakdown of marriage. Husband also may obtain divorce on grounds of wife's pregnancy at time of marriage without his knowledge or agency; wife may obtain divorce for nonsupport for two years.
Residency: Six months for plaintiff if defendant is a nonresident. Wife seeking divorce on grounds of nonsupport must have resided in the state for two years and husband and wife must have been separated during such time.

Alaska   Grounds: Impotency at time of marriage and continuing at commencement of action; adultery; conviction of felony; willful desertion for one year; cruelty impairing health or endangering life, or personal indignities rendering life burdensome; incompatibility of temperament;

*Based on Volume 7 of the *Law Digests, Uniform Acts,* A.B.A. Section of Martindale-Hubbell *Law Directory,* 1982.

drunkenness, habitual and gross, contracted after marriage and continuing for one year before commencement of action; incurable mental illness with spouse confined to an institution for at least 18 months preceding commencement of action; addiction after marriage to habitual use of drugs.
Residency: None.

Arizona Grounds: Marriage is irretrievably broken.
Residency: 90 days.

Arkansas Grounds: Adultery; impotency at time of marriage continuing to time of bringing action for divorce; desertion for one year without reasonable cause; bigamy; conviction of sodomy or infamous crime; habitual drunkenness for one year; cruel and barbarous treatment endangering life of innocent party; indignities to person of innocent party rendering his or her condition intolerable; parties have lived apart for three consecutive years without cohabitation, whether or not by mutual consent; willful nonsupport; incurable insanity of defendant confined in an institution for three years or was adjudicated to be insane for more than three years before filing suit.
Residency: Plaintiff or defendant must have resided in the state for at least 60 days.

California Grounds: Irreconcilable differences that have caused irremediable breakdown of marriage; incurable insanity.
Residency: Plaintiff or defendant must have been a resident of state for six months and of county for three months.

Colorado Grounds: Irretrievable breakdown of marriage relationship.
Residency: 90 days.

Connecticut Grounds: Marriage is broken down irretrievably or parties have lived apart for a continuous period of at least 18 months due to incompatibility; adultery; fraudulent contract; willful desertion for a year with total neglect of duty; seven years absence unheard from; habitual intemperance; intolerable cruelty; sentence to imprisonment for life; any infamous crime involving a violation of conjugal

duty and punishable by imprisonment for more than a year; or legal confinement because of mental illness for an accumulative period of at least five years.
Residency: One year.

Delaware

Grounds: Marriage is irretrievably broken because of voluntary separation; incompatibility; respondent's mental illness or misconduct; including adultery, bigamy, conviction of serious crime, desertion, physical or oral abuse of petitioning spouse or children, homosexuality, refusal to perform marriage obligations, venereal disease, habitual use of liquor or drugs.
Residency: Six months, except for misconduct for which there is no required waiting period.

District of Columbia

Grounds: Adultery; desertion for one year; voluntary separation from bed and board for one year without cohabitation; final conviction of a felony and sentence for not less than two years, partly or wholly served.
Residency: Six months.

Florida

Grounds: Marriage is irretrievably broken or mental incompetence of a party if adjudged incompetent for a preceding period of at least three years.
Residency: Six months.

Georgia

Grounds: Relationship between parties is such that marriage is prohibited; mental incapacity at time of marriage; impotency at time of marriage; force, menaces, duress, fraud in obtaining marriage; pregnancy at time of marriage unknown to husband; adultery; willful and continued desertion by either party for one year; conviction of offense involving moral turpitude with penalty two years or more in penitentiary; habitual intoxication; cruelty; incurable mental illness for two years; habitual addiction to a narcotic depressant or a stimulant drug; an irretrievably broken marriage.
Residency: Six months.

Hawaii

Grounds: Marriage is irretrievably broken, reconciliation not having been effected; voluntarily living separate and apart continuously for two years or more.
Residency: Six months.

Idaho	Grounds: Adultery; extreme cruelty; willful desertion; willful neglect; habitual intemperance; conviction of felony; permanent insanity provided insane spouse has been confined to an insane asylum in any state for at least three years; parties have continuously lived separate and apart without cohabitation for five years or more; irreconcilable differences. Residency: Six weeks.
Illinois	Grounds: Impotency; bigamy; adultery; desertion for one year without reasonable cause; habitual drunkenness for two years; attempt on life by spouse by poisoning or other means showing malice; extreme and repeated mental or physical cruelty; conviction of felony or infamous crime; infection of spouse with venereal disease; excessive use of addictive drugs for two years. Residency: Three months.
Indiana	Grounds: Irretrievable breakdown; conviction of felony subsequent to marriage; impotency existing at time of marriage; incurable insanity for two years or more. Residency: Six months, and resident of county where filed for three months.
Iowa	Grounds: Breakdown of marriage relationship to extent that legitimate objects of matrimony have been destroyed and there remains no reasonable likelihood that relationship can be preserved. Residency: One year.
Kansas	Grounds: Incompatibility; failure to perform material marital duty or obligation; incompatibility by reason of mental illness or incapacity (requires finding of confinement of spouse in institution for mental illness for two years). Residency: 60 days.
Kentucky	Grounds: Irretrievable breakdown of marriage relationship. Residency: 180 days.
Louisiana	Grounds: Adultery; conviction of a felony and sentence to death or to imprisonment at hard labor; habitual intem-

perance; excess cruel treatment, or outrages if conduct renders living together insupportable; public defamation; abandonment; attempt on the life of the other; when spouse is charged with a felony, flees from justice, and other spouse can prove guilt; intentional nonsupport; separation for one year without reconciliation; voluntary separation for six months.

Residency: Immediate divorce for adultery or conviction of felony and sentence to death or imprisonment at hard labor. One year for all other grounds, except six months for living continuously separate and apart.

Maine

Grounds: Impotence; adultery; extreme cruelty; desertion continued for three consecutive years; gross and confirmed habits of intoxication from use of intoxicating liquor, or drugs; nonsupport where one spouse being of sufficient ability to provide for other, grossly, wantonly, or cruelly refuses or neglects to provide suitable maintenance; cruel and abusive treatment; or marital differences that are irreconcilable.

Residency: Six months.

Maryland

Grounds: Any cause rendering marriage null and void or *ab initio* under Maryland's law; adultery; abandonment for at least 12 months without reasonable expectation of reconciliation; voluntary separation without cohabitation for one year; conviction of felony or misdemeanor and sentence of at least three years or indeterminate sentence in penal institution, 12 months of which have been served; uninterrupted separation without cohabitation for three years; permanent and incurable insanity, provided insane spouse has been confined in institution for not less than three years prior to suit.

Residency: One year.

Massachusetts

Grounds: Adultery; impotency; utter desertion continued for one year prior to filing of complaint; gross and confirmed habits of intoxication caused by involuntary, excessive use of liquor or drugs; cruel and abusive treatment; gross and cruel failure to support on part of spouse; irretrievable breakdown of marriage; sentence to confinement for life or five years or more in penal institution or penal reformatory institution.

Residency: If ground is irretrievable breakdown and parties file jointly, six months after court approval of agreement; otherwise, one year.

Michigan

Grounds: Breakdown of marriage to extent that objectives of matrimony have been destroyed and there is no reasonable likelihood that marriage can be preserved.
Residency: 180 days.

Minnesota

Grounds: Irretrievable breakdown of marriage relationship.
Residency: 180 days.

Mississippi

Grounds: Natural impotency; adultery unless with collusion or condonation; sentence to penitentiary unless pardoned before being sent there; desertion for one year; habitual drunkenness; habitual excessive use of drugs; habitual cruel and inhuman treatment; insanity or idiocy at time of marriage unknown to complaining party; bigamy; pregnancy by person other than husband at time of marriage, unknown to husband; consanguinity within prohibited degrees; incurable insanity for three years.
Residency: Six months.

Missouri

Grounds: Court finds no reasonable likelihood that marriage can be preserved, therefore, marriage is irretrievably broken.
Residency: 90 days.

Montana

Grounds: Marriage is irretrievably broken. Findings must be supported by evidence that parties have not lived together for 180 days prior to proceeding or that serious marital discord adversely affects attitude of one of parties.
Residency: 90 days.

Nebraska

Grounds: Finding by court that marriage is irretrievably broken.
Residency: One year.

Nevada

Grounds: Insanity existing for two years prior to commencement of action; living separate and apart and without cohabitation for one year; incompatibility.
Residency: Six weeks.

| New Hampshire | Grounds: Impotency; extreme cruelty; conviction of a crime punishable by imprisonment for more than one year and actual imprisonment under such conviction; adultery; treatment such as to seriously injure health or seriously endanger reason; absence unheard of for two years; habitual drunkenness for two years; joining any religious sect or society that professes to believe relation of husband and wife unlawful, and refusal to cohabit for six months; abandonment and refusal to cohabit for two years; willing absence of either party for two years without consent of other; when husband is willfully absent from wife for two years together, without making suitable provision for her support and maintenance; when wife of any citizen has gone to reside beyond the limits of the state, and remained absent from her husband for two consecutive years without his consent, and without returning to claim her marriage rights; when wife of any alien or citizen of any other state, living separate, has resided in state for two years together, her husband having left the United States with the intention of becoming a citizen of some foreign country and not having, during that period, come to the state to claim his marital rights, and not having made suitable provisions for his wife's support and maintenance; irreconcilable differences that have caused irremediable breakdown of marriage.
Residency: One year. |

New Hampshire

Grounds: Impotency; extreme cruelty; conviction of a crime punishable by imprisonment for more than one year and actual imprisonment under such conviction; adultery; treatment such as to seriously injure health or seriously endanger reason; absence unheard of for two years; habitual drunkenness for two years; joining any religious sect or society that professes to believe relation of husband and wife unlawful, and refusal to cohabit for six months; abandonment and refusal to cohabit for two years; willing absence of either party for two years without consent of other; when husband is willfully absent from wife for two years together, without making suitable provision for her support and maintenance; when wife of any citizen has gone to reside beyond the limits of the state, and remained absent from her husband for two consecutive years without his consent, and without returning to claim her marriage rights; when wife of any alien or citizen of any other state, living separate, has resided in state for two years together, her husband having left the United States with the intention of becoming a citizen of some foreign country and not having, during that period, come to the state to claim his marital rights, and not having made suitable provisions for his wife's support and maintenance; irreconcilable differences that have caused irremediable breakdown of marriage.

Residency: One year.

New Jersey

Grounds: Adultery; willful and continued desertion for 12 or more months; extreme cruelty, provided that no complaint for divorce on this ground shall be filed until after three months from date of last act of cruelty complained of, the proviso does not apply to counterclaim; separation, provided that husband and wife have lived separate and apart in different habitations for at least 18 consecutive months and there is no reasonable prospect of reconciliation; voluntary induced addiction or habituation to any narcotic drug or habitual drunkenness for 12 or more consecutive months, subsequent to marriage and next preceding filing of complaint; institutionalization for mental illness for 24 or more consecutive months, subsequent to marriage and next preceding filing of complaint; imprisonment of defendant for 18 or more consecutive months after marriage, provided that if parties commenced after defendant's release, parties have not resumed cohabita-

tion; deviant sexual conduct, voluntarily performed by defendant without consent of plaintiff.
Residency: One year except in the case of adultery.

New Mexico Grounds: Adultery, cruel or inhuman treatment, abandonment or incompatibility.
Residency: Six months.

New York Grounds: Cruel and inhuman treatment such that conduct of defendant so endangers physical or mental well-being of plaintiff as renders it unsafe or improper to cohabit; abandonment by defendant; neglect or refusal of defendant husband to provide for wife; adultery.
Residency: One year.

North Carolina Grounds: Adultery; natural impotency at time of marriage and still continuing; pregnancy of wife by another at time of marriage, without knowledge of her husband; continuous separation for one year; separation for three or more years without cohabitation by reason of incurable insanity of one spouse; crime against nature; bestiality.
Residency: Six months.

North Dakota Grounds: Adultery; extreme cruelty; willful temperance; conviction of a felony; insanity for five years; irreconcilable differences; willful desertion; neglect; and habitual intemperance. Willful desertion, neglect and habitual intemperance must have continued for one year in order to constitute ground.
Residency: One year.

Ohio Grounds: Bigamy; willful absence of adverse party for one year; adultery; impotency; extreme cruelty, fraudulent contract; any gross neglect of duty; habitual drunkenness; imprisonment of adverse party in penitentiary under sentence at time of filing petition; procurement of divorce outside of state, by either spouse, by virtue of which party who procured it is released from the obligations of marriage, while some remain binding upon other party; when parties have lived apart without cohabitation for an uninterrupted period of one year.
Residency: Six months.

Oklahoma	Grounds: Abandonment for one year; adultery; impotency; pregnancy of wife at time of marriage by another; extreme cruelty; fraudulent contract; incompatibility; habitual drunkenness; gross neglect of duty; imprisonment under sentence for felony at time petitions filed; procurement of final divorce decree outside of state, which does not in this state release the other party of the obligations of the marriage; insanity for five years. Residency: Six months.
Oregon	Grounds: Circumstances justifying annulment or irreconcilable differences between parties that have caused an irremediable breakdown of marriage. Residency: If parties were married in the state and suit is on grounds specified in Oregon Statutes, residence or domicile of either party in state at time suit is commenced is sufficient, otherwise one party must be resident continuously for six months prior to filing.
Pennsylvania	Grounds: One-year desertion; adultery; cruel and barbarous treatment; bigamy; conviction of serious crime; indignities rendering condition intolerable and life burdensome; confinement in mental institution for at least three years prior to filing and when there is no reasonable foreseeable prospect of discharge during the next three years; irretrievably broken marriage, either 90 days after filing complaint with mutual consent or upon three-year separation without mutual consent. Residency: Six months.
Puerto Rico	Grounds: Adultery; conviction of felony that may involve the loss of civil rights; habitual drunkenness or a continued and excessive use of opium, morphine, or any other narcotic; cruel treatment or grave injury; abandonment for over a year; absolute, perpetual, and incurable impotency occurring after marriage; attempt of husband or wife to corrupt their sons or prostitute their daughters and to connive in such corruption or prostitution; proposal of husband to prostitute his wife; separation of spouses for uninterrupted period of more than two years; incurable insanity if it seriously prevents spouses living together spiritually. Divorce by mutual consent not provided for by statute, but recognized by case law in cases where there are no children.

Residency: Plaintiff must have resided for one year, unless grounds for divorce arose in Puerto Rico while one of the spouses resided there.

Rhode Island

Grounds: Absolute divorce from bonds of marriage may be granted when marriage was originally void or voidable by law; or in case either party is, for crime, deemed to be or treated as if civilly dead; impotency; adultery; extreme cruelty; willful desertion for five years of either of parties, or for such desertion for a shorter period of time in discretion of court; continued drunkenness; habitual, excessive, intemperate use of opium, morphine, or chloral; neglect and refusal for period of at least one year before filing of petition, on part of husband, to provide necessaries for subsistence of his wife, husband being of sufficient ability; and any other gross misbehavior and wickedness, in either of parties, repugnant to and in violation of marriage covenant; or, in discretion of court when parties have lived separate and apart for a space of at least five years, whether voluntary or involuntary; or if parties have irreconcilable differences which have caused irremediable breakdown of marriage.
Residency: One year.

South Carolina

Grounds: Adultery; desertion for a period of year; physical cruelty; continuous separation for a period of one year; habitual drunkenness, habitual drunkenness to be construed to include habitual drunkenness caused by use of any narcotic drugs.
Residency: One year.

South Dakota

Grounds: Adultery; extreme cruelty; willful desertion, willful neglect; habitual intemperance; conviction for felony; incurable chronic mania or dementia of either spouse, having existed for five years or more; willful desertion, willful neglect, habitual intemperance must have continued for one year.
Residency: No specific time; plaintiff must be resident of or stationed in state.

Tennessee

Grounds: Either party of marriage is impotent; either party has knowingly entered into a second marriage, previous one still subsisting; adultery; willful and malicious desertion with absence for one year without reasonable cause; conviction of an infamous 'crime; conviction of a crime that is a felony under the laws of the state and sentenced to the penitentiary; attempts on life of other by means showing malice; refusal by husband or wife, without reasonable cause, to remove to this state and willfully absenting himself or herself for two years; woman was pregnant at time of marriage by another without husband's knowledge; habitual drunkenness or abuse of narcotic drugs contracted after marriage.

Residency: No length of residence required where acts were committed while plaintiff was a bona fide resident of state and is so at time of filing suit. Divorce may be granted upon proper grounds arising out of state, while petitioner resided out of state, provided petitioner or defendant has resided in state six months next preceding filing of bill.

Texas

Grounds: Divorce may be granted in favor of either spouse when other is guilty of cruel treatment against complaining spouse, if such ill treatment is of such nature as to render living together insupportable; other has voluntarily left complaining spouse for one year with intention of abandonment; adultery; living separate and apart without cohabitation for three years; convicted after marriage of felony and imprisoned, provided that no suit of divorce will be sustained on this ground until 12 months after final judgment of conviction and not then if convicted spouse has been pardoned or was convicted on testimony of complaining spouse; confined to mental hospital for three years; marriage has become insupportable because of discord or conflict of personalities that destroys legitimate marriage relationship and prevents any reasonable expectation of reconciliation.

Residency: Six months and resident of county where suit is filed for preceding 90 days.

Utah

Grounds: Impotency at time; adultery; willful desertion for more than one year; willful neglect to provide common necessaries of life, thus willful neglect; habitual drunkenness; conviction of felony; cruelty causing bodily injury or great mental distress; permanent insanity, legally adjudged; separation for three years under decree of separate maintenance.

Residency: Three months of state and county.

Vermont	Ground: Adultery; confinement at hard labor in state prison for at least three years if defendant is actually confined at the time of bringing the libel; intolerable severity; willful desertion or absence for seven years without being heard of; failure of either spouse to provide suitable maintenance, if able to do so, and without cause persistently refuses or neglects to do so; either husband or wife is incurably insane and confined for at least five years; if married persons have lived separate and apart from spouse for six consecutive months and resumption of marital relations is not reasonably probable. Residency: Six months, except ground of insanity must be two years.
Virginia	Grounds: Sodomy/buggery committed outside marriage; adultery; conviction of either party of a felony and confinement for more than one year: cruelty (after one year of separation for such act); for willful desertion after one year; one year of separation without any cohabitation; or after six months of separation without cohabitation if there are no minor children. Residency: Six months.
Virgin Islands	Grounds: When there has been a breakdown of marriage relationship to the extent that legitimate objects of matrimony have been destroyed and there remains no reasonable likelihood that marriage can be preserved. Residency: Six weeks.
Washington	Grounds: Petition by either or both parties that the marriage is irretrievably broken. Residency: Petitioner must be resident at time of filing or member of armed forces stationed in Washington.
West Virginia	Grounds: Adultery; final conviction of felony after marriage; willful abandonment or desertion for six months; cruel and inhuman treatment; habitual drunkenness; habitual use of narcotic or dangerous drugs; parties living separate and apart in separate places of abode without cohabitation without interruption for one year; permanent incurable insanity where individual has been confined in mental hospital for three years. Residency: One year.

91

Wisconsin	Grounds: Both parties petition or otherwise under oath confirm marriage is irretrievably broken; one party states parties have lived voluntarily apart continuously for one year next preceeding commencement of action; if only one party so states and parties have not lived voluntarily apart one year court either finds no prospect of reconciliation or after court finds prospect of reconciliation and adjourns hearing, at adjourned hearing either party states under oath or affirmation that marriage is irretrievably broken. Residency: Six months.
Wyoming	Grounds: Irreconcilable differences in marital relationship; and when either person has become incurably insane and confined in mental hospital at least two years before action commenced. Residency: 60 days.

Part 2:
The Forms–
How To File Your
Divorce

(On the ground of Voluntary Separation Without Cohabitation)

It is not recommended that you proceed to file your own divorce without an attorney because there can be so many pitfalls. Even if you want to do it yourself, you should at least consult an attorney to review the papers you are filing. The $50 or $100 that you spend for a consultation may save you months in time, aggravation, and money.

The Forms	Following are sample forms for the District of Columbia,* Maryland, and Virginia. Some forms can be obtained directly from the court or clerk's office, while others have to be typed up. *The forms are in filing sequence and are numbered only for your convenience.* You must refer to the forms by the names on the samples when discussing your case with the court clerks or hearing commissioners. Before you start, it would be advisable to review several recent divorce cases, which you can get from the clerk's office. Reading the cases can give you a more comprehensive view of how divorce cases are handled.

Although the wording of the forms varies by jurisdiction, there are four essential steps, or forms, to every divorce case. They are the Bill of Complaint, the Proof of Service, the Answer, and the Final Decree or Judgment. |
The Complaint	The Complaint is filled out by the person who is called the plaintiff or petitioner. The plaintiff is the person who starts or brings the divorce action to a court of law. The tags of "plaintiff" and "defendant" are legal assignations and have nothing to do with guilt in an uncontested divorce action, on the ground of voluntary separation without cohabitation.
The Answer	The Answer is the paper filled out and filed by the defendant. It informs the court that the defendant is aware of the suit and gives him or her the opportunity to respond to it. In the District of Columbia an Answer must be filed. In Maryland a decree Pro Confesso often is filed in lieu of an Answer, and filing a Waiver rather than an Answer is common practice in Virginia.
Service	Service is the process by which your spouse is notified that you have initiated a suit for divorce. To complete service, you will need patience, forms, and often a kindly court clerk to help you fill in the forms if you have any problems. Keep in mind that court clerks are prohibited from giving you any legal advice, which would be practicing law without a license.
The Final Decree	The Final Decree also is known as the Judgment, the Findings of Fact, and the Conclusions of Law. It is the most important part of your divorce. It's the paper that says the court has heard all the evidence and either agrees with or denies your divorce action.

Forms to Type Yourself*	*Forms Obtainable from the Court*
Form 1, the Complaint	Form 2, the Summons
Form 4, the Answer	Form 3, U.S. Marshal's Service and Process Record
Form 7, the Judgment	Form 5, Praecipe for an alias summons
	Form 6, Uncontested Praecipe

1. The first step is to fill out Form 1, the Bill of Complaint.

2. Have the Complaint notarized by a notary public.

3. Make at least three copies of the Complaint. Be sure to have one for your personal records.

4. File the original copy of the Complaint with the Court Clerk at 451 Indiana Avenue, N.W., at the Superior Court of the District of Columbia. Pay the $45 filing fee, and ask the clerk for the Summons and the U.S. Marshal's Service and Process Record. Fill both in according to the directions. You can also file two Summonses, one to be served at your spouse's home address, the other to be served at work. If you are sending service to one address only, in the boxes of the U.S. Marshal's Service Form "No. of Total," you would write in "one of one." But if you are sending two copies of the Summons, write in "one of two" in the boxes, as shown in the sample.

5. You must attach one copy of your Complaint with each Summons you order.

6. The marshal has 20 days in which to serve your spouse. If service is completed, a copy of the Instruction and Process Record form titled "Notice of Service" will be sent to you, indicating the date, location, and time that your spouse was served. You'll also be notified if the marshal wasn't able to serve the Summons.

7. If your spouse was served successfully on the first attempt, he or she is given 20 days in which to file an Answer.

8. If service wasn't obtained, you must go back to the court and file another Summons and U.S. Marshal's Service Instruction and Process Record. The only change is under the heading "Type of Writ" on the U.S. Marshal's form. Write "alias summons" in that block. At the same time, ask the clerk for Form 5, a Praecipe, and write, "Please issue an alias summons in the above-captioned

*D.C. requires forms to be typed on 8½″ × 13″ traditional legal paper.

matter." Sign it, followed by *prq se* and your address. There's an additional charge of one dollar for the marshal each time an alias summons is issued.

9. If your spouse was served and hasn't filed an Answer within 20 days, you can go back to the court and ask that an attorney be appointed to represent your spouse. There's a $100 charge for the court-appointed attorney, which you and your spouse must pay in advance. (Lawyers have the power to hold up divorce cases until they are paid.) The lawyer will contact your spouse and file an Answer with the court.

10. After an Answer is filed, file the Uncontested Praecipe, Form 6. Sign your name, followed by *pro se,* and have your spouse's attorney sign it. The clerk will assign a court date, which you and your spouse's attorney will be notified of by mail. Call the lawyer to confirm the date. If he or she doesn't show up, the hearing will be postponed.

11. Fill out the Judgment, Form 7, and bring it with you to the hearing. Remember to also bring a certified copy of your marriage certificate with you to the hearing.

How to File in Md.

Forms to Type Yourself*

Form 1, the Complaint
Form 2, the Answer
Form 3, Motion for Decree Pro Confesso
Form 4, Military Affidavit
Form 5, Decree Pro Confesso
Form 6, Line
Form 7, Decree of Divorce

Forms Obtainable from the Court

Form 8, Maryland State Department of Health and Mental Hygiene's Report of Absolute Divorce or Annulment of Marriage

1. Type Form 1, the Complaint, according to the sample.

2. Have the Bill of Complaint notarized by a notary public. Make three copies of the Complaint.

3. File the original copy with the Court Clerk and ask that a Summons be issued. The filing fee is $60, plus $5 for the sheriff's service. A copy of the Complaint also has to be given to the sheriff.

4. Give the clerk a self-addressed post card and on the back, write: Sheriff's return _____; Defend-

*Maryland requires forms to be typed on 8½" × 11" paper.

ant served on _____. The Sheriff will mail the post card back to you, indicating whether or not service was obtained; and if so, when, where, and at what time.

5. The defendant then has a court-designated period of time (which varies) in which to file an Answer, Form 2.

6. If service wasn't obtained, you have to file a Line, Form 6, with the clerk, which would read, "Please issue an alias summons in the above-captioned matter." There is an additional charge of $5, payable to the sheriff of the county in which your spouse is residing.

7. If your spouse has filed an Answer, then you both must fill out, sign, and file Form 6, the Line. Write, "The above-captioned matter is uncontested as to all issues." Pay the master's fee—which varies by county—and a hearing date will be set.

8. If your spouse hasn't filed an Answer within the designated period of time, you must file Form 3, Motion for Decree Pro Confesso and Form 4, Decree Pro Confesso. Both are filed at the same time. The defendant must fill in the Military Affidavit, which is filed with the Motion for Decree Pro Confesso.

9. If the Order is granted, the judge will sign the Decree Pro Confesso and a court date will be set. You do not have to file a Line, Form 6, if you are filing a Decree Pro Confesso.

10. Type up Form 7 and get Form 8 from the clerk's office. Fill in according to samples and bring them with you to court for your hearing.

How to File in Va.	*Forms to Type Yourself**	*Forms Obtainable from Clerk*
	Form 1, the Complaint	Form 3, Subpoena in Chancery
	Form 2, the Waiver	Form 6, Commonwealth of Virginia report of Divorce or Annulment
	Form 4, the Decree of Reference	
	Form 5, the Judgment	

NOTE: Form 4, the Decree of Reference varies by jurisdiction. The one in the sample is for Alexandria City. Check recent divorce cases at the Clerk's office to find the specific wording for your jurisdiction.

1. Fill in Form 1, the Complaint, which you do not have to have notarized.

2. Make four copies of the Complaint.

---

*Virginia requires forms to be typed on 8½″ × 11″ paper.

3. File the original plus two copies with the Court Clerk (keep the fourth copy for your personal files). Filing fees will vary from approximately $32.50 to $37.50.. Inclusive in the fee is the sheriff's service, which is Form 3, the Subpoena in Chancery. The Clerk also will assign a number to your case, which is as important as your phone or social security number. In the future, always refer to your case by the number. While you're at the Clerk's office, ask for Form 6, the Commonwealth of Virginia Report of Divorce or Annulment. Fill it in and ask the Clerk to include it in your file.

4. The defendant has 21 days in which to respond to the Bill of Complaint after service was obtained. Service may take as long as two weeks.

5. Wait approximately two weeks and then call the Clerk to find out whether or not service was obtained.

6. If service wasn't obtained (although it usually is, since Virginia law allows for "posting" the Subpoena and Complaint on the defendant's door if no one is home), go back to the court and ask to have an alias summons issued.

7. The defendant should file a Waiver, Form 2, which is in lieu of an Answer. The Waiver, in effect, agrees to the allegations contained in the Complaint and asks that the case be expedited as soon as possible. Most lawyers and parties to the divorce action prefer the Waiver because it really does speed up the process.

8. After a Waiver has been filed, call the Clerk to make sure that it is in your file.

9. The next step is to file a Decree of Reference, Form 5, with the Clerk. Write a note to the Clerk asking that the Decree be sent to a judge for entry. Sign your name and give your address.

10. Wait a week or two, call the Clerk and ask which Commissioner in Chancery has been assigned to your case.

11. Call the Commissioner to set up a time and date for your hearing.

12. Bring your witness and two checks with you to the hearing. Commissioner fees will range from $50 to $75 and the court reporter (who is usually the Commissioner's secretary) will charge from $35 to $45. When setting up the hearing date with the Commissioner, ask in advance if there will be a court reporter there. You may have to hire your own.

13. After the hearing, the Commissioner will file a report with the Clerk and notify you of the filing time. It

could take two days to two years, but count on two weeks.

14. After the Commissioner's report is filed, mail your Judgment , Form 5, to the Court Clerk and ask that it be sent to a judge for signing. The judge should sign it within a few days. You are now what is theoretically called "a free person."

Sample Forms for the District of Columbia, Maryland, and Virginia

Note: These forms are samples. If you plan on doing your own District of Columbia divorce, the forms should be typed on legal (8½ × 13 inches) bond paper, with the double red vertical margins. The paper can be bought from any office supply store. Forms for Maryland and Virginia must be typed on 8½″ × 11″ paper.

FORM 1 (D.C.) SUPERIOR COURT OF THE DISTRICT OF COLUMBIA
Family Division
Domestic Relations Branch

Your full name

Your street address

City, State, Zip Code

Plaintiff

v.

Spouse's full name

Spouse's street address

City, State, Zip Code

Defendant

Court Clerk will
Civil Action No. _assign number_

COMPLAINT FOR ABSOLUTE DIVORCE
(Six months Voluntary Separation)

Comes now the plaintiff, _Your full name_ , pro se,
and respectfully represents to this Honorable Court as follows:

(1) That the jurisdiction of the Court is based on Title 11, Section 1101
of the District of Columbia Code (1981 Ed.) and on Title 16, Section 904 of the
District of Columbia Code (1981 Ed.)

(2) That plaintiff is an adult citizen of the United States and is a
bona-fide resident of the District of Columbia, and has been for more than six
months next preceding the filing of the Complaint.

(3) That defendant is an adult citizen of the United States and a
resident of _state of residence_ .

(4) That on _date of marriage_ the plaintiff and the defendant
were lawfully married in the _state and county you were married in_ .

(5) That no children were born of this marriage.

(6) That plaintiff and defendant, herein, lived and cohabited together as
husband and wife until _date you separated_ when they mutually and voluntarily agreed
to live separate and apart without cohabitation. The parties have mutually and
voluntarily continued to live separate and apart without cohabitation beginning
with the date aforestated, and said separation has continued through the present time.

102

(7) That since the separation of the parties, the plaintiff has resided at

list all addresses since your separation: street no., apt #, city and state, zip

and the defendant has resided at ___*same as above, but for defendant*___

(8) That there is no hope of reconciliation.

(9) That the wife's maiden name is ___*fill in wife's maiden name*___

and that she desires to resume using her maiden name and that such use will not

constitute a fraud on any person.

WHEREFORE, the premises considered, the plaintiff prays:

(1) That *s/he* be awarded an absolute divorce on the grounds that the part-

ies have mutually and voluntarily lived separate and apart without cohabitation

for a period of six months next preceding the commencement of the action.

(2) ___*FOR WOMEN ONLY: if desired add "That her maiden name of (give full maiden name) be restored to her."*___

(3) For such other and further relief as to the Court may seem just and

proper. *↖ (2) if second paragraph is not used.*

Plaintiff's signature
Print or type name above
Plaintiff, <u>pro se</u>
Plaintiff's full address

VERIFICATION

DISTRICT OF COLUMBIA, SS: *FILL IN ONLY IN PRESENCE OF A NOTARY*

I, _____, being first duly sworn on oath depose

and say that I have read the foregoing Complaint, by me subscribed, and that the

contents thereof are true to the best of my knowledge, information and belief.

_____
Plaintiff

Subscribed and sworn to me on this _____day of _____

_____
Notary Public

My commission expires_____.

FORM 2 (D.C.)

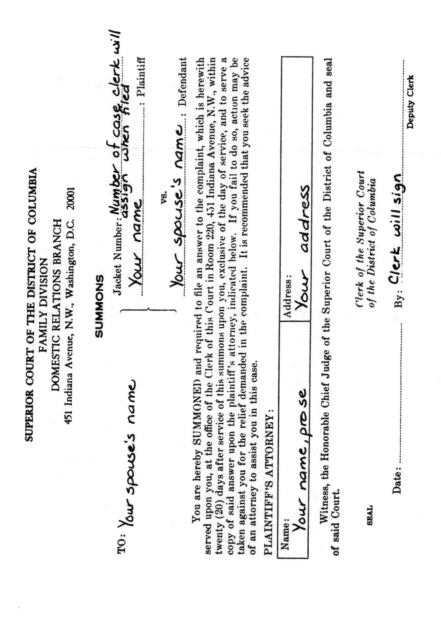

SUPERIOR COURT OF THE DISTRICT OF COLUMBIA
FAMILY DIVISION
DOMESTIC RELATIONS BRANCH
451 Indiana Avenue, N.W., Washington, D.C. 20001

SUMMONS

Jacket Number: *Number of case clerk will assign when filed*

Your name : Plaintiff

vs.

Your spouse's name : Defendant

TO: *Your spouse's name*

You are hereby SUMMONED and required to file an answer to the complaint, which is herewith served upon you, at the office of the Clerk of this Court in Room 220, 451 Indiana Avenue, N.W., within twenty (20) days after service of this summons upon you, exclusive of the day of service, and to serve a copy of said answer upon the plaintiff's attorney, indicated below. If you fail to do so, action may be taken against you for the relief demanded in the complaint. It is recommended that you seek the advice of an attorney to assist you in this case.

PLAINTIFF'S ATTORNEY:

Name:	Address:
Your name, pro se	*Your address*

Witness, the Honorable Chief Judge of the Superior Court of the District of Columbia and seal of said Court.

Clerk of the Superior Court
of the District of Columbia

SEAL

Date: _____ By: *Clerk will sign*

Deputy Clerk

104

FOR USE OF U.S. MARSHAL OR PROCESS SERVER

I hereby certify and return that I served the within Summons and Complaint upon

Name: _____

Address: _____

on the _____ day of _____, 19___ at _____ AM/PM

☐ Personally.

☐ Individual served is a person of suitable age and discretion then abiding in the defendant's usual place of abode.

☐ I further certify that defendant is not a resident of the District of Columbia.

☐ I hereby certify and return that after diligent investigation I am unable to serve the individual, company, corporation, etc., named above.

Dates of Endeavor and/or Remarks: Time: _____ AM/PM

OFFICE OF THE U.S. MARSHAL   By: _____
DISTRICT OF COLUMBIA   Signature of Marshal Representative

PROCESS SERVER'S CERTIFICATION

I hereby certify that I am a competent person over eighteen years of age residing or maintaining a regular place of business in the District of Columbia with no interest in the subject matter of this suit nor am I a party thereto and that I have served this SUMMONS and COMPLAINT as indicated[2] above.

Signature of Process Server: _____ Age: _____

Business Address: _____

Residence: _____

Subscribed and sworn to before me this _____ day of _____, 19___

_____
Notary Public
District of Columbia

_____
(Deputy Clerk)

FORM 3 (D.C.)

U.S. MARSHALS SERVICE
PROCESS RECEIPT and RETURN

INSTRUCTIONS: See "INSTRUCTIONS FOR SERVICE OF PROCESS BY THE U.S. MARSHAL" on the reverse of the last (No. 5) copy of this form. Please type or print legibly, insuring readability of all copies. Do not detach any copies.

PLAINTIFF	COURT NUMBER
Your name	*Case number*
DEFENDANT	TYPE OF WRIT(S)
Your spouse's name	*Summons*

SERVE NAME OF INDIVIDUAL, COMPANY, CORPORATION, ETC., TO SERVE OR DESCRIPTION OF PROPERTY TO SEIZE OR CONDEMN

Your spouse's name

ADDRESS (Street or RFD, Apartment No., City, State and ZIP Code)

Your spouse's address

SEND NOTICE OF SERVICE COPY TO NAME AND ADDRESS BELOW:

Your name
Your complete address

Number of writs to be served with this form-285	*one of one* or *one of two*
Number parties to be served in this case	*one*
Check for service on U.S.A.	*not applicable*

SPECIAL INSTRUCTIONS OR OTHER INFORMATION THAT WILL ASSIST IN EXPEDITING SERVICE:

Fill in best time to serve your spouse.

Signature of Attorney or other Originator requesting service on behalf of: ☐ PLAINTIFF ☐ DEFENDANT

TELEPHONE NUMBER *Your phone*

DATE *Date of filing*

Your name pro se

SPACE BELOW FOR USE OF U.S. MARSHAL ONLY – DO NOT WRITE BELOW THIS LINE

Total Writs	District of Origin	District to Serve	Signature of Authorized USMS Deputy or Clerk	Date

I acknowledge receipt for the total number of writs indicated (Sign only first USM 285 if more than one 285 is submitted)

I hereby certify and return that I ☐ have personally served, ☐ have legal evidence of service, ☐ have executed as shown in "Remarks", the writ described on the individual, company, corporation, etc., at the address shown above or on the individual, company, corporation, etc., at the address inserted below.

☐ I hereby certify and return that I am unable to locate the individual, company, corporation, etc., named above. (See remarks below)

Name and title of individual served (if not shown above)

☐ A person of suitable age and discretion then residing in the defendant's usual place of abode.

Date of Service	Time	
		am pm

Address (complete only if different than shown above)

Signature of U.S. Marshal or Deputy				
	Forwarding Fee	Service Fee	Mileage (including endeavors)	Total

REMARKS:

1. CLERK OF THE COURT

FORM 4 (D.C.) SUPERIOR COURT OF THE DISTRICT OF COLUMBIA
Family Division

Plaintiff's full name
and your full address
v.

Defendant's full name
and spouse's full address

Civil Action No. Court Clerk will assign number

ANSWER

Comes now the defendant, Defendant's full name

appearing pro se, and answers as follows:

(1) Defendant admits all of the allegations of paragraphs 1, 2, 3, 4, 5, 7, 8, and 9 of the Complaint filed herein.

(2) Defendant neither admits nor denies the allegations of paragraph 6 of the Complaint, but demands strict proof thereof.

Defendant's signature

Pro se
Defendant's full address

NOTARY will FILL IN THIS PART   VERIFICATION

Then appeared before me _____ who affirmed to me
his or her
that the foregoing was true to the best of h̶i̶s̶ knowledge and belief and sub-

scribed before me this _____ day of _____, 19 ___.

Notary will sign

Notary Public

CERTIFICATE OF SERVICE

I certify that a copy of this Answer was served upon Plaintiff by mailing
it to _____ Plaintiff's full name and address

postage prepaid, this ___DATE___ day of ___month___, 19 ___Year___.

Defendant's signature
PRINT OR TYPE DEFENDANT'S NAME

FORM 6 (D.C.)

PRAECIPE

Superior Court of the District of Columbia

DOMESTIC RELATIONS BRANCH

THE ___Date___ DAY OF ___Month___, 19 ___Year of filing___

___Your name___

vs.

___Your spouse's name___

No. ___Case Number___

The Clerk of said Court will please note that the above entitled cause is, in fact

UNCONTESTED AS TO ALL ISSUES. _____

_____

_____

_____

___Your signature pro se___
Attorney for Plaintiff

___Your spouse's or spouse's attorney's signature___
Attorney for Defendant

FORM DR-47/Jan 72

109

FORM 5 (D.C.)

SUPERIOR COURT OF THE DISTRICT OF COLUMBIA
FAMILY DIVISION
DOMESTIC RELATIONS BRANCH

PRAECIPE

Jacket No. _Case Number_

Date: _Date of filing_

Your name
(Plaintiff)

vs.

Your spouse's name
(Defendant)

The Clerk of said Court will _____

110

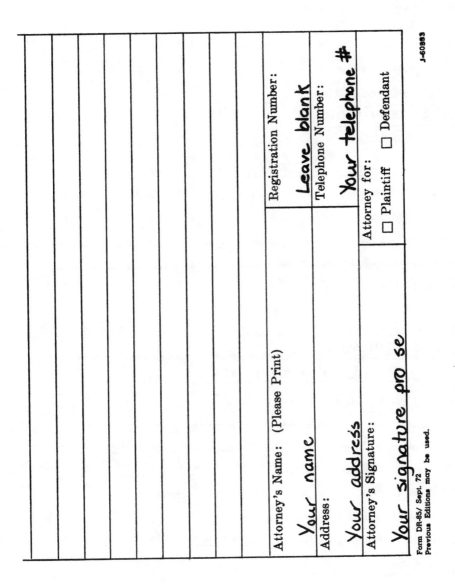

Attorney's Name: (Please Print)

Your name

Address:

Your address

Attorney's Signature:

Your signature pro se

Registration Number:

Leave blank

Telephone Number:

Your telephone #

Attorney for:

☐ Plaintiff   ☐ Defendant

Form DR-85/ Sept. 72
Previous Editions may be used.

J-60893

111

FORM 7 (D.C.) SUPERIOR COURT OF THE DISTRICT OF COLUMBIA
Family Division

Your full name
Your street address
City, State, zip Code

_____
Plaintiff

v.

Spouse's full name
Spouse's street address
City, State, zip Code

_____
Defendant

Civil Action No. Court Clerk will assign number

JUDGMENT OF ABSOLUTE DIVORCE,
FINDINGS OF FACT, CONCLUSIONS OF LAW AND ORDER

This cause came on for hearing on the complaint for absolute divorce filed by the plaintiff herein; that on the basis of the present hearing, the testimony of the parties and their witnesses adduced therein, the plaintiff and the defendant appearing pro se, the Court hereby enters the following findings of fact, conclusions of law and order.

FINDINGS OF FACT

(1) The parties were married on the ___date___ day of ___month___ 19 Year in the ___state where married___ , and of this union no children were born.

(2) That on or about ___date of separation___ the plaintiff and the defendant voluntarily separated; that the said separation has continued voluntarily, uninterrupted and without cohabitation to the present date, that since the separation of the parties the plaintiff has lived at ___address since separation___ and that the defendant has lived at ___defendant's address since separation___

(3) That there are no property rights to be adjudicated or adjusted herein.

(4) That there is no hope of a reconciliation.

(5) That the wife's maiden name is ___fill in wife's full maiden name___ and that she desires to be restored to that name.

112

(6) That the plaintiff and the defendant voluntarily separated on or about __date of separation__ , and that the plaintiff is therefore now entitled to an absolute divorce from the defendant on the ground of voluntary separation for more than six months without cohabitation.

(7) That the wife is now entitled to the full use and restoration of her maiden name.

WHEREFORE, the premises considered, it is this ___date___ day of ___month___ 19 _Year_,

ADJUDGED, ORDERED and DECREED:

(1) That the plaintiff, __Plaintiff's full name__ , be and is hereby granted an absolute divorce from the bonds of matrimony existing between h_his or her_self and defendant __Defendant's full name__ , on the ground of voluntary separation without cohabitation.

(2) FOR WOMEN ONLY: if desired add, "That the maiden name of (Your full maiden name) be restored to the wife."

IT IS FURTHER ORDERED

That the judgment herein shall not be effective until the expiration of the time allowed for the taking of an appeal, or until the final disposition of any appeal, if taken.

Judge will sign
_____
Judge

I hereby recommend adoption of the foregoing findings of fact and conclusions of law.

Commissioner will sign
_____
Commissioner

The undersigned parties hereby waive the provisions of Family Division Rule (D.)

Plaintiff's signature   Defendant's signature
_____   _____
Plaintiff   Defendant

113

FORM 1 (Md.)   IN THE CIRCUIT COURT FOR THE COUNTY OF *County where filing*

THE STATE OF MARYLAND
Sitting in Equity

Your full name
Your street address
City, State, Zip code
　　　　Plaintiff

v.

Spouse's full name
Spouse's street address
City, State, Zip code
　　　　Defendant

Equity No. *Court clerk will assign number*

BILL OF COMPLAINT FOR DIVORCE A VINCULO MATRIMONII
(12 Months Voluntary Separation)

TO THE HONORABLE, THE JUDGES OF SAID COURT:

The plaintiff, *your full name*, respectfully represents to this Honorable Court as follows:

(1)   That the plaintiff is an adult *male / female* citizen of the United States and a resident of the county of *county you reside in*, State of Maryland, and has for more than one year immediately preceding the filing of this Bill of Complaint been a resident of the State of Maryland.

(2)   That the defendant is an adult *male / female* citizen of the United States, and is a resident of *state*.

(3)   That the plaintiff and the defendant were lawfully married on *date of marriage* in the *state where wedding took place*

(4)   That no children were born of this marriage.

(5)   That the plaintiff and the defendant have lived voluntarily separate and apart without any cohabitation and without interruption for a period of more than one year prior to the filing of this complaint. Said parties commenced living separate and apart on *date of separation* which has continued without cohabitation or interruption until the present and there is no hope or possibility of a reconciliation.

114

WHEREFORE, plaintiff prays:

(1) That(s)he may be granted a divorce <u>a vinculo matrimonii</u> from the defendant,

(2) *For women only: "That her maiden name of (your full maiden name) be restored to her."*

And to such other and further relief as to the Court may seem just and proper.

Your signature

Plaintiff, <u>pro se</u>

STATE OF MARYLAND :
: ss. *This section filled in by Notary Public*
COUNTY OF _____:

I HEREBY CERTIFY that on this _____ day of _____,

19____, before me, the subscriber, a notary public in and for the State and

County aforesaid, personally appeared _____ and made

oath in due form of law that the matters and facts set forth in the foregoing

Bill of Complaint are true to the best of his/her knowledge, information and

belief.

IN WITNESS WHEREOF, I hereunto set my hand and official seal.

_____
Notary Public

My Commission Expires:

_____

FORM 2 (Md.)

IN THE CIRCUIT COURT FOR ___County where filing___ COUNTY, MARYLAND
Sitting in Equity

Your full name
Your street address
City, State, Zip code
Plaintiff

v.

Equity No. *Court clerk will assign number*

Spouse's full name
Spouse's street address
City, State, Zip code
Defendant

ANSWER TO BILL OF COMPLAINT
FOR DIVORCE A VINCULO MATRIMONII

TO THE HONORABLE, THE JUDGE OF SAID COURT:

The Defendant, ___Name___, respectfully represents unto this Honorable Court, in Answer to Bill of Complaint For Divorce A Vinculo Matrimonii

(1) That (s)he admits the allegation contained in paragraph 1 of the Bill of Complaint.

(2) That (s)he admits the allegation contained in paragraph 2 of the Bill of Complaint.

(3) That (s)he admits the allegation contained in paragraph 3 of the Bill of Complaint.

(4) That (s)he admits the allegation contained in paragraph 4 of the Bill of Complaint.

(5) That (s)he admits the allegation contained in paragraph 5 of the Bill of Complaint.

116

WHEREFORE, the Defendant prays:

(1) That the Plaintiff be granted the relief sought in the Bill of Complaint.

(2) And for such other and further relief as the nature of this cause may require or to this Honorable Court may deem just and proper.

And as in duty bound, etc.

Defendant's signature

VERIFICATION

I do solemnly declare and affirm under the penalties of perjury that the matters and facts set forth in the foregoing Answer to Bill of Complaint For Divorce A Vinculo Matrimonii by me subscribed, are true and correct.

Defendant's signature

CERTIFICATE OF SERVICE

I HEREBY CERTIFY that a copy of the foregoing Answer to Bill of Complaint For Divorce A Vinculo Matrimonii was mailed, postage prepaid, this *date* day of *month*, 19*year*, to: *Plaintiff or Plaintiff's attorney's name*.

Defendant's signature

FORM 3 (Md.)

IN THE CIRCUIT COURT FOR _County where filing_ COUNTY, MARYLAND
Sitting in Equity

Your full name
Your street address
City, State, Zip code
                    Plaintiff

v.   Equity No. _Court clerk will assign number_

Spouse's full name
Spouse's street address
City, State, Zip code
                    Defendant

MOTION FOR DECREE PRO CONFESSO

Comes now the Plaintiff, _Name_, and respectfully request this Court to issue a decree pro confesso and in support thereof states the following:

(1) That the Defendant, a resident, whose residence address is _Defendant's address_.

(2) That on the _date_ day of _month_, 19_year_, the Defendant was served with the Bill of Complaint by the Sheriff at _____ _____.

(3) That the Defendant has failed to appear or answer this Court in person or by solicitor within the time prescribed by the said Summons.

WHEREFORE, your Plaintiff respectfully requests this Court to issue a decree pro confesso granting the Plaintiff leave to take testimony before the Master for Domestic Relations for the Circuit Court for _County_ County, Maryland, to support the allegations of the Bill of Complaint.

Plaintiff's signature, pro se

FORM 4 (Md.) IN THE CIRCUIT COURT FOR _County where filing_ COUNTY, MARYLAND

Sitting in Equity

Your full name
Your street address
City, State, Zip code
Plaintiff

v.

Equity No. _Court clerk will assign number_

Spouse's full name
Spouse's street address
City, State, Zip Code
Defendant

MILITARY AFFIDAVIT

STATE OF MARYLAND :
:
COUNTY OF _____ :

Notary will complete this section

_____ _Plaintiff's name_ _____, being first duly sworn, on oath deposes and says that ___he is the Plaintiff in the above entitled cause and that ___he has caused a careful investigation to be made to ascertain whether or not the above named Defendant, _Defendant's name_, is in the military service of the United States, and that as a result of his investigation affiant has discovered and does hereby allege that said Defendant, _Defendant's name_, is not in the Military Service of the United States, and was not nor has she been a member of the Military Service of the United States during pendency of this action, that is to say said Defendant is not a member of the Army of the United States, the United States Navy, the Marine Corps, the Coast Guard, and is not an officer of the Public Health Service detailed by proper authority for duty either with the Army or Navy, and said Defendant is not on active duty with any of the branches aforesaid.

Notary will complete and sign

Plaintiff's signature

SUBSCRIBED and SWORN to before me this _____ day of _____, 19___.

_____
Notary Public

My Commission Expires:

_____

119

FORM 5 (Md.)   IN THE CIRCUIT COURT FOR _County where filing_____ , COUNTY, MARYLAND
Sitting as a Court of Equity

_Your full name_____
_Your street address_____
_City, State, Zip code_____
                Plaintiff

v.   Equity No. _Court clerk will assign number_

_Spouse's full name_____
_Spouse's street address_____
_City, State, Zip code_____
                Defendant

DECREE PRO CONFESSO

Upon consideration of the Plaintiff's Motion for Decree Pro Confesso,
and it appearing that the Defendant has been served with process and a copy
of the Bill of Complaint in the above entitled cause, and (s)he having failed
to file an Answer thereto within the time allowed for pleading to said cause, it
is, by the Circuit Court for _County_____ , County, Maryland, this _____
day of _____ , 19____ , _Judge will complete_

ADJUDGED, ORDERED AND DECREED, that leave be granted to the Plaintiff to
take testimony before one of the Standing Examiners in Chancery to this Court
to support the allegations of the Bill of Complaint. It is further ordered that
the Bill of Complaint be and the same is hereby taken Pro Confesso.

_Judge will sign_____
                Judge

Master, Domestic Relations Causes
Master, Domestic Relations _will sign_
        Causes

120

FORM 6 (Md.)

IN THE CIRCUIT COURT FOR _County where filing_ COUNTY, MARYLAND
Sitting in Equity

Your full name.
Your street address
City, State, Zip code
       Plaintiff

v.

Equity No. _Court clerk will assign number_

Spouse's full name.
Spouse's street address
City, State, Zip code
       Defendant

<u>LINE</u>

Mr. Clerk,

    Please enter the above captioned matter as Uncontested as to all issues.

Plaintiff's signature   _Defendant's signature_

FORM 8 (Md.)

THIS FORM MUST BE FILED WITH YOUR JUDGMENT.

ADDITIONAL COPIES CAN BE OBTAINED FROM THE CLERK'S OFFICE.

MARYLAND STATE DEPARTMENT OF HEALTH AND MENTAL HYGIENE
Division of Vital Records
301 West Preston Street
Baltimore, Maryland 21201

REPORT OF ABSOLUTE DIVORCE OR ANNULMENT OF MARRIAGE

HUSBAND

1. NAME (First) (Middle) (Last) Complete Items 1-19.	2. AGE	3. Place of Birth (State or foreign country)
4. RESIDENCE (City) (County) (State)	5. Number of this Marriage (First, Second, Third)	6. Race White ☐ Negro ☐ Other ☐ (Specify)........

WIFE

7. MAIDEN NAME (First) (Middle) (Last)	8. AGE	9. Place of Birth (State or foreign country)
10. RESIDENCE (City) (County) (State)	11. Number of this Marriage (First, Second, Third)	12. Race White ☐ Negro ☐ Other ☐ (Specify)........

MARRIAGE PARTICULARS

13. Place of this marriage (County) (State or foreign country)	14. Date of this Marriage (Month) (Day) (Year)

15. Plaintiff Husband ☐ Wife ☐	16. Decree granted to 1. Husband ☐ 2. Wife ☐	17. Legal grounds for decree	18. Total number of living children .... No. under 18 years of age .....

19. Name of Attorney for Plaintiff (Street Address) (City or Town) (County) (State)

122

CLERK OF CIRCUIT COURT

Docket No.	Folio No.		Type of Decree: 1. Absolute (A Vinculo) ☐ 2. Annulment ☐

I hereby certify that the above persons were divorced and decree signed on:

(Month)   (Day)   (Year)

Name of Clerk of Court	Signature of Clerk of Court	County of Decree

INSTRUCTIONS: TO THE CLERK OF THE CIRCUIT COURT: When a petition for absolute divorce or annulment is filed, please hand a copy of this form to the attorney for completion of items No. 1 through 19. When the decree is signed check completeness of these items, execute the bottom section and mail to Maryland State Department of Health, Division of Vital Records, 301 W. Preston Street, Baltimore, Maryland 21201 on or before the 10th of the month next succeeding the divorce.

TO THE ATTORNEY: Please complete items No. 1 through No. 19 of the Report of Absolute Divorce or Annulment of Marriage and ask your client to verify the information. RETURN THE FORM TO THE CLERK OF THE COURT FOR CERTIFICATION.

DHMH-21
VR A24 7/74 25M

123

FORM 7 (Md.)

IN THE CIRCUIT COURT FOR _County where filing_ COUNTY, MARYLAND
Sitting as a Court of Equity

Your full name
Your street address
City, State, Zip Code
      Plaintiff

v.

    Equity No. _Court Clerk will assign number_

Spouse's full name
Spouse's street address
City, State, Zip Code
      Defendant

DECREE OF DIVORCE
(A Vinculo Matrimonii)

This cause being presented for determination; testimony having been taken before the Domestic Relations Master of this Court

on _____ day of _____ 198__, and the said Master having filed his report, findings and recommendations, and the entire proceedings having been considered, it is this _____ day of _____, 19__, by the Circuit Court for _____ County, Maryland, sitting as a Court of Equity, **JUDGE WILL FILL OUT THIS PART**

    ADJUDGED, ORDERED and DECREED, that the Plaintiff, _Your name_,

be, and (s)he hereby is, divorced a vinculo matrimonii from the Defendant, _Spouse's name_ .

Judge will sign
JUDGE, Circuit Court for
_____ County, Maryland

THIS IS A PROPER DECREE TO BE PASSED:
Domestic Relations Master will sign
Domestic Relations Master

APPROVED AS TO FORM AND CONTENT:
Defendant's signature
Plaintiff's signature

FORM 1 (Va.)

IN THE CIRCUIT COURT OF THE COUNTY OF _County where filing_

Your full name
Your street address
City, State, Zip Code
Complainant

v.

Spouse's full name
Spouse's street address
City, State, Zip Code
Defendant

IN CHANCERY NO. _Court Clerk will assign number_

BILL OF COMPLAINT

COMES NOW your Complainant, _Your name_ ,
pro se, and in support of _his/her_ Bill of Complaint respectfully represents
as follows:

1. That the Complainant, _Your name_ , and the defendant,
were lawfully married on May 3 1975 in Boynton Beach, Florida.

2. That both parties are over the age of eighteen (18) years and neither
is a member of the Armed Forces of the United States.

3. That there were no children born of this marriage.

4. That the Complainant has been domiciled in and has been an actual bona
fide resident of this state for more than six (6) months next preceding the
commencement of this suit.

5. That the Defendant is also a resident of the State of Virginia and is
currently residing in _name of county_ .

6. That the parties have lived separate and apart without interruption and
without any cohabitation for more than one (1) year, to-wit: _date of separation_ ;
and that there is no hope of a reconciliation between the parties.

7. For Women only: if desired add "That her maiden name of (your full maiden name) be restored to her."

WHEREFORE, your Complainant, _____ your name

prays that _s/he_ may be awarded a divorce a vinculo matrimonii on the ground of one (1) year separation; and that _s/he_ be awarded such other and further relief as the nature of _his/her_ cause may require.

Print or type your name
Sign here
Your street address
City, State, Zip Code

FORM 2 (Va.)

IN THE CIRCUIT COURT FOR THE COUNTY OF *County where filing*

Your full name
Your street address
City, State, Zip code
     Complainant

v.

IN CHANCERY NO. *Court clerk will assign number*

Spouse's full name
Spouse's address
City, State, Zip code
     Defendant

WAIVER

STATE OF VIRGINIA

COUNTY OF _County_____, to wit:

    This day personally appeared *Plaintiff's name*

before the undersigned notary public in and for the city and state aforesaid,

and, having been first duly sworn according to law, deposes and states as

follows: that (s)he is the defendant in the above cause; that (s)he waives

all further notice of proceedings herein, including the taking of

depositions and the entry of any decreed or orders herein, and hereby

consents to the immediate maturity of this cause for hearing.

Defendant's signature

Notary will complete this section

SUBSCRIBED and SWORN to before me this _____ day of

_____, 19___.

                        _____
                        Notary Public

                        My Commission expires: _____

Commonwealth of Virginia

IN THE CIRCUIT COURT OF THE COUNTY OF ARLINGTON

SUBPOENA IN CHANCERY

Clerk will fill out.

The party upon whom this writ and the attached paper are served is hereby notified that unless within twenty-one (21) days after such service, response is made by filing in the Clerk's Office of this court a pleading in writing, in proper legal form, the allegations and charges may be taken as admitted and the court may enter a decree against such party, without further notice, either by default or after hearing evidence.

Appearance in person is not required by this subpoena.

Done in the name of the Commonwealth of Virginia, this............day of................................, 19..........

...., CLERK.

...., DEPUTY CLERK.

...., p. q.

(OFFICE ADDRESS)

FORM 4 (Va.)

IN THE CIRCUIT COURT FOR THE CITY OF ALEXANDRIA

Your full name
Your street address
City, State, Zip code
      Complainant

                                                      Court clerk will
                              IN CHANCERY NO. *assign number*

v.

Spouse's full name
Spouse's street address
City, State, Zip code
      Defendant

DECREE OF REFERENCE

THIS CAUSE came to be heard upon the papers formerly read and upon motion of the Complainant, pro se, that this case be referred to a Special Commissioner in Chancery for a hearing; and it appearing to the Court that this cause has duly matured for a hearing, upon consideration wherefore, it is hereby   *Judge will complete*

ADJUDGED, ORDERED and DECREED that this cause be referred to _____, who is hereby directed to take testimony and report the same, pursuant to the Order heretofore entered by this Court on the _____ day of _____ 19__, recorded in Chancery Book No. 28 at page 187.

ENTERED this _____ day of _____, 19__.

                                       Judge will sign
                                     Judge

I ASK FOR THIS:

Your signature

FORM 5 (Va.)

IN THE CIRCUIT COURT OF THE COUNTY OF *County where filing*

Full name only
_____
Complainant

v.

Full name only
_____
Defendant

IN CHANCERY NO. *Court clerk will assign number*

DECREE OF DIVORCE A VINCULO MATRIMONII

This case came to be heard upon the Bill of Complaint; upon service of process upon the defendant in *state where defendant lives* by the Deputy United States Marshall on *date of service*; upon proof of service and return filed with this court on *date proof of service was filed with court clerk*, no Answer having been filed by the defendant; upon the depositions in behalf of the complainant duly taken and filed herein; upon the report of *name of Commissioner in Chancery who heard your case* one of the Commissioners in Chancery of this Court, to whom this cause was referred by Decree of Reference entered herein on *date decree was filed* and upon argument of the complainant.

And it appearing to the Court, independently of the admissions of either party in the pleadings or otherwise, that the parties hereto were married on *date of marriage* at *city and state where marriage took place* that no children were born of the marriage; that both parties are members of the *Caucasian, Black, Oriental* race, are sui juris, and neither party is a member of the Armed Forces of the United States; that at the time of filing of this suit the complainant was and had been a bona fide resident of and domiciled in the County of *County complainant resides in*, State of Virginia, and had been such a resident and so domiciled for more than six months next preceding the filing of this suit; that the parties last lived and cohabitated as husband and wife in *County last resided in as husband + wife* County, Virginia; that the parties separated on *date of separation* while they were residing at *full street address, city, state*, and since that

130